Workbook 3

Understanding Business Process Management

Institu... ...amme

 the Institute of Management
FOUNDATION

Pergamon
Open
Learning

Pergamon Open Learning
An imprint of Butterworth-Heinemann
Linacre House, Jordan Hill, Oxford OX2 8DP
225 Wildwood Avenue, Woburn, MA 01801-2041
A division of Reed Educational and Professional Publishing Ltd

℞ A member of the Reed Elsevier plc group

OXFORD   AUCKLAND   BOSTON
JOHANNESBURG   MELBOURNE   NEW DELHI

First published 1997
Reprinted 1998, 1999

British Library Cataloguing in Publication Data
A catalogue record for this book is available from the British Library

ISBN 0 7506 3659 9

Typeset by Avocet Typeset, Brill, Aylesbury, Bucks
Printed and bound in Great Britain

FOR EVERY TITLE THAT WE PUBLISH, BUTTERWORTH-HEINEMANN
WILL PAY FOR BTCV TO PLANT AND CARE FOR A TREE.

Contents

Series overview

The Institute of Management Open Learning Programme is a series of workbooks prepared by the Institute of Management and Pergamon Open Learning for managers seeking to develop themselves.

Comprising seventeen open learning workbooks, the programme covers the best of modern management theory and practice, and each workbook provides a range of frameworks and techniques to improve your effectiveness as a manager, thus helping you acquire the knowledge and skill to make you fully competent in your role.

Each workbook is written by an experienced management writer and covers an important management topic or theme. The activities both reinforce learning and help to relate the generic ideas to your individual work context. While coverage of each topic is fully comprehensive, additional reading suggestions and reference sources are given for those who wish to study to a greater depth.

Designed to be practical, stimulating and challenging, the aim of the workbooks is to improve performance at work by benefiting you and your organization. This practical focus is at the heart of the competence based approach that has been adopted by the programme.

The structure of the programme

The design and overall structure of the programme has two main organizing principles, both of which are closely linked to the national standards for management developed by the MCI (Management Charter Initiative).

First, the workbooks are grouped according to the key roles of management.

- Underpinning the management standards are a series of **personal competences** which describe the personal skills required by all managers, which are essential to skill in all the main functional or key role areas.
- **Manage Activities** describes the principles of managing processes and activities, with service to the customer as an essential part of this.
- **Manage Resources** describes the acquisition, control and monitoring of financial and other resources.
- **Manage People** looks at the key skills involved in leadership, developing one's staff and managing their performance.

- **Manage Information** discusses the acquisition, storage and use of information for communication, problem solving and decision making.

In addition, there are three specialized key roles: **Manage Quality, Manage Projects** and **Manage Energy**. The workbooks cover the first two of these. Unlike the four primary key roles above, these are not compulsory for certificate, diploma or S/NVQ requirements, but provide options for the latter.

Together, these key roles provide a comprehensive description of the fundamental principles of management as it applies in any organization – commercial, maintained sector or not-for-profit.

Second, the programme is organized according to **levels of management**, seniority and responsibility.

Level 4 represents first line management. In accredited programmes this is equivalent to S/NVQ Level 4, Certificate in Management or CMS. Level 5 is equivalent to middle/senior management and is accredited at S/NVQ Level 5, Diploma in Management or DMS. There are two S/NVQs at Level 5: Operational Management and Strategic Management. The operations role is focussed internally within an organization on the maintenance of systems and standards of output, whilst the strategic role is focussed on the whole organization, including the external operating environment, and looks at setting directions.

Together, the workbooks cover all the background knowledge you need to have for all units of competence in the MCI standards at Level 4 and Level 5 (apart from the specialized units in the key role Manage Energy). They also provide skills development and opportunities for portfolio building.

For a comprehensive list of workbooks, see page ix. For a comprehensive list of links with the standards, see the *User Guide.*

How to use the programme

The programme is deliberately designed to be flexible and can be used in a variety of ways:

- to update on important management topics and themes, or develop individual skills: as the workbooks are grouped according to themes, it should be easy for you to pick out one that suits your needs

- as part of generic management development programmes: you can choose the modules that fit the themes of the programme

■ **as part of, and in support of, accredited competence-based programmes.**

For N/SVQs at both Levels 4 and 5, there are options in the combinations of units that make up the various awards. By using the map provided in the *User Guide*, individuals will be able to select the workbooks appropriate to their specific needs, and their chosen accreditation options. Some of the activities will help you provide evidence for your portfolio; where we think this is the case, we give the relevant reference to the standards.

For Certificate or CMS, Diploma or DMS, individuals should choose modules that not only meet their individual needs but also satisfy the requirements of the delivering body and the awarding body.

You may need help and guidance in these choices, and the *User Guide* sets out the options and advice in much more detail. A fuller description of the potential uses of this material in evidence gathering and portfolio building can also be found in the *User Guide*, as can a detailed description of the contents of each workbook.

Workbooks in the Institute of Management Open Learning Programme

An asterisk indicates that a particular workbook also contains material suitable for a particular key role or personal competence over and above that where it is principally designated.

Links to qualifications

S/NVQ programmes

This workbook can help candidates to achieve credit and develop skills in the key role of Manage People and covers the following units and elements:

A4   Contribute to improvements at work
A4.1   Improve work activities
A4.2   Recommend improvements to organizational plans

Likewise, it will also help candidates to achieve credit and develop skills in the key role Manage Quality and covers the following units and elements:

F4   Implement quality assurance systems
F4.1   Establish quality assurance systems
F4.2   Maintain quality assurance systems
F4.3   Recommend improvements to quality assurance systems

Certificate and Diploma programmes

This workbook, together with the other Level 4 workbook on managing activities (4 – *Customer Focus*) covers all of the knowledge required in the key role Manage Activities for Certificate in Management and CMS programmes.

Links to other workbooks

Other workbooks in the key role managing activities at Level 4 are:

Introduction

Who is it for?

This workbook is for you if...

- you are managing in a changing – and increasingly demanding – market environment
- your organization is implementing Total Quality Management
- you want to improve the efficiency of activities and reduce waste
- you want to increase cost-effectiveness and the value your operation adds
- you need to get to grips with processes and systems in a new role
- you are starting a new operation from scratch

What's in it for you?

In this workbook, we explore the concept of business processes. What are they, and why do you need to know? What can they do for you, and how do you do it? Finally, how can you ensure they deliver, and what are the implementation issues to watch?

Practically everything we do can be recast as a process; planning a holiday, writing a letter, cooking a meal. In the organizational context, processes are the activities that turn inputs (raw materials, resources, staff effort) into outputs (goods or services) that the customer wants. In other words, processes are the way we add value.

The concept has long been used in manufacturing to focus efforts on streamlining and enhancing the efficiency of production processes. But increasingly, what differentiates organizations is not their products, but their service. So the process approach is now being applied more widely to service processes in the organization – to administrative, sales, marketing, human resource, strategic decision making, and management processes – where the customer may be internal or external to the organization.

The concept of processes is fundamental to a number of the most influential management trends in recent years – Total Quality Management and Continuous Improvement (or Kaizen); Business Process Re-engineering and Business Process Redesign. Processes may even provide the subject matter for teambuilding and empowerment initiatives geared at getting people to take greater responsibility for their own performance.

The durability and flexibility of the concept proves its worth. This is not just another management fad, influenced by the latest magazine article or visiting management consultant. It takes us back to basics. If the organization is in business to deliver value-added goods and services, how we do this is central to the organization's success. A prime source of competitive advantage derives from managing processes to deliver goods and services more efficiently, more effectively, and more responsively.

The tools and techniques of process management can help you to manage the activities in your operation – to plan, delegate, progress, monitor and improve them. But we are still talking about tools and techniques, not magic wands. Analysing something won't necessarily improve it. The most efficient process in the world is useless if no one will operate it. And it's no good having just one world-class process in an otherwise mediocre operation. What you deliver to your customers may depend on tens or even hundreds of interlocking processes. While you cannot expect to achieve world class in every one of these, the chain is only as strong as its weakest link.

This workbook is intended as a practical roadmap, leading you through the jargon and the key ideas to help you anticipate and evaluate the implications of implementing ideas for your operation and the organization as a whole. You will find case studies and examples illustrating how other organizations have applied the concepts. And you will work through structured activities to build your own expertise in using the essential tools and techniques in your own organization.

Objectives

By the end of this workbook you should be able to:

- identify the contribution of business processes to the organization's work
- trace the link between processes and quality assurance
- apply techniques to improve business processes
- establish systems to monitor quality

Section 1   What's involved?

In this section of the workbook, we consider what processes are and what they are for. We review the external pressures affecting organizations, and link these to the emergence of process management and total quality approaches. We pose three fundamental questions at the heart of process management and introduce a seven-step framework for process improvement. Finally, we introduce the recommendations of process practitioners for clearly defined process roles and responsibilities.

When you have worked through this section of the workbook, you should be able to:

- identify processes and what they contribute to the organization
- identify factors that affect this contribution
- recognize the link with quality
- recall one approach to managing processes
- recognize the different roles and responsibilities in process structures

What is a process?

The *New Shorter Oxford English Dictionary* defines a process as:

... a continuous series of actions, events or changes ... especially a continuous and regular action or succession of actions occurring or performed in a definite manner; a systematic series of actions or operations directed to some end.

So a process involves a number of **activities** or **transformations**, which are organized into a **specific sequence** and co-ordinated to achieve a **specific end** (or output). A process can be represented diagrammatically as shown in Figure 1.

For example, the process of booking your holiday might involve the following **activities**:

- discuss preferences
- research the possibilities
- draw up a shortlist
- make a decision
- book the holiday

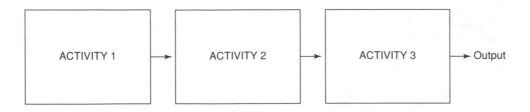

Figure I   A simple process

The **order** of the activities is significant – you wouldn't be able to book the holiday until you'd made a decision; and you wouldn't be able to draw up a shortlist until you'd researched the possibilities. To enable you to complete the activities, you'd require a number of **inputs** to the process, such as travel brochures (information), a pen and paper for the shortlist (tools and materials) and the money to pay for the holiday (funding). The **ouput** of the process is the holiday reservation. Figure 2 illustrates the process of booking a holiday.

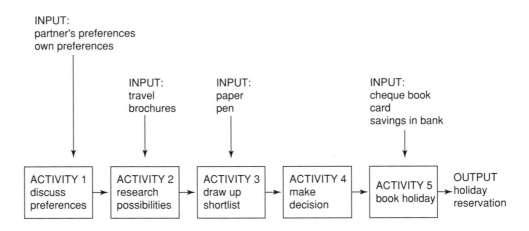

Figure 2   Booking your holiday

Business processes

A business process is any process (including all the activities and all associated inputs) that an organization must carry out to deliver outputs to its customers. It doesn't matter whether yours is a profit-making or non-profit organization, public or private sector, large or small, you will achieve your objectives through processes of one sort or another. For example, in a hospital, processes might include diagnosing medical problems, carrying out essential surgery, and treating disease; the output would be a healthy patient. A publisher's processes might include commissioning, typesetting, and printing a book (the eventual output).

The writers and practitioners in business processes point out that there may be hundreds or even thousands of processes in an organization. However, even in the large multinational organizations there may be as few as twenty to thirty 'macro' processes. These are the major processes that operate the business and deliver outputs to customers, but each step of a macro process may be a smaller process in its own right. The smaller process can be broken down into activities, and these activities into tasks, and so on. So processes may be 'nested' like Russian dolls, one inside another.

ACTIVITY 1

Take a few moments to list the main outputs that your operation delivers. Name the processes associated with each output (e.g. booking a holiday, assembling a product, providing advice or information, collecting payment, solving customers' problems). Don't worry about the individual activities at this stage – we'll come to those later.

Output   **Processes**

HORIZONTAL THINKING

You may have found it tempting to list your processes in terms of the functional areas or workgroups that perform them. Perceptions of activities are often strongly influenced by the traditional hierarchical structure of a functional organization – as seen on a thousand organization charts near you and illustrated in Figure 3. In this kind of set-up, information, authority and decisions flow vertically up and down each function. Interfaces between functions may be less well developed. The problem is that most processes flow horizontally.

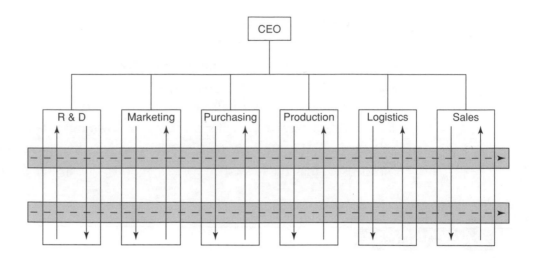

Figure 3   Functional hierarchy and the flow of processes

What is a process for?

Processes enable the organization to:

- achieve the organization's objectives, and
- deliver outputs for customers

The processes that deliver actual goods and services directly to your **external customers** are the **core** processes. However, you may be unable to achieve these outputs without other processes within the organization – for example, resourcing, to ensure you have the staff to carry out the activities; purchasing, to buy the materials, tools and equipment inputs; or accounting, to manage the money required to stay in business. This second type of process is a **support** process. Support processes usually deliver their outputs to an **internal customer** – someone else inside the organization, who then uses these outputs in their own activity or process. In Figure 4, the output of the picking process (the items that were selected) becomes the input of the wrapping process.

Figure 4   Process for order fulfilment from stock

A third type of process provides the framework through which people can achieve everything else. This is an **infrastructure** process, for example, setting and communicating the organization's mission, policies, values and strategies; leading and managing people; developing the business structure. These processes co-ordinate and direct activities, to minimize duplication and help everyone to pull in the same direction.

Figure 5 illustrates how the three types of process fit together.

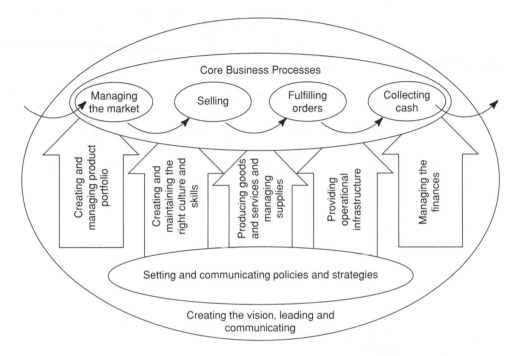

Figure 5   Three types of process

How you categorize your processes may vary from organization to organization. For example, if you are in retailing, you may consider the purchasing process core to your business. Selling may seem less central in a public service operation such as a library or a local council. It may also be difficult to decide quite where one process ends and another begins. Does the process of launching a new product start when you research the customer need, when you develop the product, or when you plan the customer launch?

ACTIVITY 2

How do the processes you listed in Activity 1 relate to Figure 5? Which are
core, which support, and which provide the infrastructure?

Type of process	Process description
Core	
Support	
Infrastructure	

How does Figure 5 help you understand the processes in your organization?

FEEDBACK

Obviously, we can't comment on how you categorized your processes; talk it over with a
colleague if you find this helpful. You may have found that Figure 5 emphasizes the
interdependence of many of these processes, which may be less obvious when you're in the
middle of operating them from day to day.

For example, the arcane processes of the information technology section of a
large insurance company might seem rather distant from the output delivered to customers. However, difficulties or improvements in the IT capability
may have a significant impact on the core processes (assessing risk, selling
insurance, arranging cover, dealing with payments or progressing claims).
The skills required to assess risk without computers, for example, might be
very different. You would probably appoint a different kind of person and
their training would be quite different. At the same time, without computers,
misjudgements could be more likely; and the organization might lose out on
poor risks. This in turn might increase the costs of insurances to customers.

Why manage processes?

If processes exist to enable the organization to achieve its objectives, and deliver outputs that customers want, then the better you do both these things, the greater your competitive advantage. The greater your competitive advantage, the more successful the organization is likely to be. But there are a number of factors working against you here, and this is why processes require management. The goalposts are constantly moving. Hannagan (1995) highlights four factors exerting pressure on organizations today:

1   **Turbulence**   We live in turbulent times. The rate and scale of change in the marketplace, the economy, politics, society, legislation and the environment is relentless. What customers want and need is constantly changing. Even if your process was once world class, standing still while others around you adapt or anticipate means that you are losing competitive advantage.

2   **Technology**   Automation, miniaturization, computerization, electronic communication: advances in technology have radically reshaped the way we work. Some jobs are redundant; others are created. Things are moving so fast that some equipment is obsolete before it reaches the organization. The organization with the latest equipment may have an instant advantage. For example, Figure 6 illustrates the rate of change in transport. For thousands of years, since humans first stood on their hind legs, the top speed at which humans could travel remained relatively unchanged – the speed they could run, or the speed of a horse, or carriage. Then, little more than 150 years ago, as steam power and then the combustion engine were invented, things hotted up;

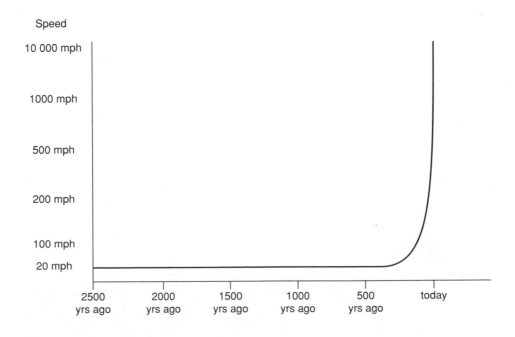

Figure 6   Rate of change in transport

in the last fifty years, speed has increased exponentially. Today we have rockets that can reach Mars and even ordinary mortals travel on planes that are faster than the speed of sound.

3   **Time**   Timespans for everything have shortened dramatically. It takes seconds to access information that used to require a lengthy search; electronic communication is practically instantaneous; product and service life cycles have shrunk to a fraction of what they were. Success depends not just on developing the right product or service, but on getting it to market quickly. It's not just a question of dealing with change, it's doing it NOW.

4   **Interdependence**   We touched on this in the last activity, but as the environment changes, as technology improves, and as timescales shorten, interdependence increases – across processes, functional specialisms, and even organizations. Just-in-time techniques, for example, mean that you are depending on your suppliers to get you what you need when you need it. Some tasks or roles are no longer viable in-house and must be outsourced – think of cleaning or catering in the health service, for example. So changes in any one element may have consequential ripples through the organization and beyond.

ACTIVITY 3

Identify ways in which each of the following factors have influenced your organization in the recent past.

Turbulence

Technology

Time

Interdependence

PROCESS ENTROPY

There is another reason for active management of processes: process entropy. Over time, processes degrade and become less efficient.

Most processes evolve piecemeal. They may have been designed to deliver a specific output at a particular point in time, but as requirements and circumstances change, they are modified, expanded, dispersed across several workgroups. Responsibility may become muddied, so additional checks and balances are introduced at the cross-over points. 'Patches' are applied to fix recurrent problems.

Consequently, our business processes become ineffective, out of date, overly complicated, burdened with bureaucracy, labour intensive, time consuming and irritating to management and employees alike.

(Harrington, 1991, p.17)

For example, keeping employee records might have started life as a paper-based process. Computerization was introduced, and to start with (because people weren't sure how the system would work, and wanted to check it out), the paper records were maintained side-by-side with the new system. But somehow, no one was ever ready to relinquish the checks and balances, so the paper-based records never quite died out and now people operate both systems as a matter of course.

So after a while, it's worth critically reviewing your processes – even and especially the well-established ones – to make sure that there's not a simpler way, or a more effective way, or a quicker way, to achieve the same outcome.

After you've done a thing the same way for two years, look it over carefully; after five years, look at it with suspicion; and after ten years, throw it away and start all over again.

A.E. Pearlman, US railroad executive
cited in Harrison and D'Vaz, *Business Process Re-engineering*

ACTIVITY 4

How has process entropy affected any of the processes you identified in
Activity 1?

Quality matters

The above factors have led to an increasing emphasis on quality, and initiatives such as total quality management, continuous improvement or
Kaizen.

Quality has a specific meaning in this context. It doesn't mean that the
products or services are luxury items – genuine leather and walnut; 24-carat
gold; hand crafted (or whatever). In processes, quality is a reflection of *the fit
between what customers want and what the organization delivers*. This
means that not only must the product or service conform to the specifications of the customer, but the way it is delivered must conform to requirements. It must be delivered when and where the customer wants it, and at an
acceptable price.

Customers are becoming increasingly sophisticated, discerning and
demanding. Products and services as diverse as soft drinks, computers and
satellite television have a global market. Advances in any one area soon
become the norm across the world. So increasingly, what differentiates products or services – and secures competitive advantage – is the way they are
delivered.

WHAT WAS WRONG WITH INSPECTION?

Traditional approaches to quality typically focus only on the product or service, rather than on how it is delivered. Inspection identifies and rejects products or services that are not up to scratch. But the problem is that this tends
to be too late – at the end of the process, when considerable organizational
effort has already been expended. Furthermore, unless you inspect every sin-

gle product or service delivery, some outputs that don't meet the standards are bound to slip through and reach customers.

DESIGNING QUALITY IN

With total quality approaches, how the output is created and delivered – the process – becomes the focus of attention. Quality is designed in; the process itself is optimized, specified and controlled to increase consistency and minimize unwanted variance in the output. Measurable indicators of performance are identified for each stage of the process and the output is measured against these as it moves through the process, so that there are earlier opportunities (and more of them) to spot problems, and take action. And because the checkpoints are more frequent along the way, diagnosing problems and solving them becomes more focused and less haphazard. In this way, improving the process to improve the quality of the output becomes an explicit and intrinsic element of the process.

So where do you start?

Process management begins with a fundamental reappraisal of the whys and wherefores of a process:

- why are we doing this at all?
- why do we do it in this particular way
- is there a better way to do it?

It sounds radical – and it can be. You may be challenging processes that have been enshrined in company lore for many years. The people who set them up may feel you are questioning their judgement. The people operating them may feel you are impugning their performance. And the processes themselves go to the heart of what the whole organization is about.

These questions are just the start of managing processes. Because, of course, managing processes involves more than asking questions. It means finding the answers, and deciding what to do about them. It means managing whatever action is required to ensure that the process delivers its fullest potential. It means providing leadership and support for the people who must implement the process and any improvements. And it means setting up systems to keep you on track.

A FRAMEWORK FOR PROCESS MANAGEMENT

Below is a step-by-step framework that will help you manage and improve your processes. It's not original: it's simply one proven route map, to help you keep track of where you are now and where you're heading. There are seven steps in the framework:

1 **identify critical processes** – because you may have most to gain from improving these

2 **analyse processes** – work out exactly what's involved in each, and assess how well each process is currently working

3 **evaluate opportunities for improvement** – some improvements may bring greater rewards than others; the feasibility of others may be problematic. The skill lies in distinguishing the two, and prioritizing your efforts

4 **specify targets for improvement** – because you need to know what you're aiming for

5 **plan and implement the improvement** – as you would any project

6 **review the results** – to check how the improvement has worked, and finally

7 **decide 'what next?'** – because process management is not a one-off: it's a continuous and ongoing process itself which may best be illustrated by the process improvement cycle shown in Figure 7.

Figure 7   Process management framework

ACTIVITY 5

Take a moment now to think about where you are on the seven-stage framework, and the route ahead. What concerns does this approach to managing processes raise?

NEVER-ENDING STORY?

You may feel as though process management is a treadmill. You'll never be able to sit back and enjoy the fruits of your labour – the world is constantly changing, so processes will always need to be revised, updated, improved. In fact, process management is a continuous progression or spiral. You may come round to the same kinds of activities as you review and decide next steps, but you have moved onwards and upwards. You have the satisfaction of seeing how far you have come.

Getting organized for process improvement

Most of the writers and experienced practitioners of process approaches – whether of the incremental improvement or radical re-engineering persuasion – have emphasized the importance of setting up a reporting and operating structure specifically for process activities.

If you want people to share an understanding and a commitment to the process, you have to create opportunities for them to meet, communicate, share problems, build solidarity, learn and work together. Processes may span different functional areas, different sites, and different viewpoints, even extending to your suppliers and your customers. The traditional functional hierarchy may make it difficult to communicate across the functional divides, never mind beyond the boundaries of the organization itself.

However, the average manager may have no mandate to reach across the fence and set up mixed process teams. Furthermore, the power protocol surrounding a matrix set-up, where vertical and horizontal team membership intersect, has always been problematic: who or what takes precedence (see Figure 8)?

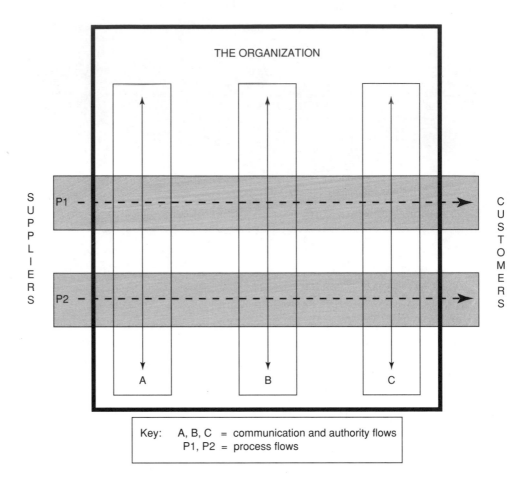

Figure 8   Who takes precedence?

A COUNSEL OF PERFECTION?

The business process experts have developed several variants of an alternative hierarchy of essential roles and responsibilities for successful process management, improvement or re-engineering. The formally instituted roles may not be immediately feasible in your organization. However, if you are operating on a process basis, even informally, you probably already have a network of people – the telephone numbers stuck on the wall by your phone, or the page in your process file, for example – who fulfil much the same kinds of role. These are your first port of call in the event of any difficulty or changes to the system.

Process champion (or sponsor)

A senior manager (preferably the chief executive) who:

■ supports and authorizes the process efforts
■ models the kinds of behaviour associated with process-led operations (focus on customer, collaboration, etc.)
■ on a practical level, ensures that resources are made available for process efforts

Steering committee (or executive improvement team)

A team of senior managers who:

■ institute the process approach
■ agree strategic priorities
■ set up the individual process improvement teams
■ maintain the overview on all process activity

Process owner

The most senior manager with a vested interest in a specific process (and a portion of whose rewards are probably linked to its success). The process owner:

■ agrees (with the process champion) the purpose and scope of improvement efforts on the process
■ assumes responsibility for the process outcome
■ agrees with the process improvement team the performance indicators (e.g. productivity) and measures (e.g. £sales per head) on which the process will be evaluated
■ co-ordinates and supports the process improvement team
■ ensures that the team acquires the skills, knowledge and understanding of the process and the necessary tools and techniques
■ progresses regular reviews and audits
■ manages and co-ordinates connections with interdependent processes

Process improvement team

The process improvement team comprises around eight people, drawn from the stakeholders throughout the process – including customers and suppliers – who specifically focus their attention on improving the process. They work to:

- document the process
- analyse current performance
- identify areas for improvement
- propose and evaluate improvements
- specify new targets and measures
- plan implementation of improvements
- review performance of improvements
- report progress to the process owner

Process operators or process team

The process operators are all the people who actually operate the process and deliver the outputs to internal and external customers. Especially in a culture of empowerment, they may have significant opportunities to:

- document any subprocesses
- identify areas for improvement
- propose improvements
- implement improvements
- review performance
- report progress to the process owner
- fulfil their process activities

ACTIVITY 6

For any major process you know, identify the personnel involved and their responsibilities. How well do their responsibilities match the role descriptions above?

Process

Person	Responsibility	Closest role description

Summary

A business process involves a series of activities that transform inputs into outputs. Core processes deliver outputs directly to the external customer and support processes enable them to do so, while infrastructure processes create the organization itself.

Quality is a reflection of the fit between what customers want and what you deliver (your output). The better the fit, the more likely it is that your organization will attract and retain customers. But external and internal pressures for change mean that the goalposts are moving. Managing processes is therefore an ongoing activity, constantly monitoring and improving to ensure that processes stay effective, efficient and responsive.

The key questions are: why are we doing this at all? Why do we do it in this particular way? And is there a better way to do it? Then it's a question of finding the answers, deciding what to do about them, planning and implementing action, and reviewing progress.

Process practitioners recommend an alternative hierarchy to facilitate process efforts and overcome the barriers to effective teamworking that may stem from traditional organizational structures. The process champion authorizes, endorses and resources the efforts. The steering committee plans and co-ordinates process efforts across the organization. The process owner is responsible for a specific process; the process improvement team works on improving it; and the process operators implement the process and deliver the outputs.

Section 2 What needs managing?

In this section of the workbook, we consider what it is that defines the quality of a process – the process itself, the people who operate it, and the systems that support it. We introduce the process scorecard which proposes indicators to help you diagnose the current capability of your process, and the potential for improvement. We identify critical processes – those that have greatest impact on your customers or on the organizational objectives. And we combine the results of the scorecard and the critical processes to identify priorities for improvement efforts.

When you have worked through this section of the workbook, you will be able to:

- identify the three dimensions of process quality
- evaluate the capability of your own processes against the process scorecard
- identify critical processes which have greatest impact on the customer or the organization's objectives
- prioritize processes for improvement efforts

Managing the fit

Processes are how the organization delivers output to the customer. The closer the fit between what the customer wants and what you deliver, the more successful you are likely to be in securing and retaining customers. But as we have seen, organizations are operating in an environment of constant change – in the marketplace, in their immediate environment, in technology, and most importantly, in what their customers want and expect from them. It is not enough simply to keep an eye on existing processes and solve the occasional problem.

The goalposts are moving; so it is a question of constantly readjusting your aim to stay on target. And this is what process management is all about.

3-D QUALITY

A process may deliver quality through three dimensions (illustrated in Figure 9):

- the **process** itself (is it effective, efficient, and responsive?)
- the **people** who operate it (do they know what they have to do, and can they do it?)
- the **systems** that support it and keep it on track (is the process documented and understood, are relevant measures established, and is feedback regularly sought?)

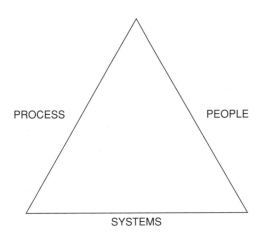

Figure 9   Three dimensions of process quality

When these three dimensions are optimized, the process delivers quality for the customer. This is the basis of the process scorecard on the pages that follow. First, we'll look at each dimension in turn.

The process

There are three criteria for a quality process: that the process should be effective, efficient and responsive.

EFFECTIVE

An effective process delivers the **right** product or service – one that actually meets the wants and needs of your customer, on time, every time. Which means that you need to find out what customers want, specify it in measurable terms, and then take steps to ensure that your output meets those specifications.

How far does the output currently meet customer needs? Are there difficulties or gaps? Is there anything they particularly value? Can they make any suggestions to improve the output in their eyes? Every interaction with the customer offers the opportunity to gather this kind of intelligence. And until you know these things directly from the customers themselves (rather than from your own gut feeling or guesswork) any efforts to improve the processes may miss the mark.

Once you know what they want, action may range from incremental improvements tweaking and fine-tuning elements of the existing process, through to radical re-engineering and restructuring, starting with a clean slate and creating an entirely new process, from the customer back through the organization. Your day-to-day efforts are probably more likely to be closer to the incremental version of continuous improvement – although even here, initial gains may still be startlingly impressive.

Effective processes are likely to result in high levels of customer satisfaction with the product or service itself.

ACTIVITY 7

Do your processes deliver the right product? How do you know?

EFFICIENT

An efficient process **optimizes** the way resources are used. It uses the fewest inputs to deliver the output to specification; activities are arranged logically; duplication and gaps are eliminated. Delays and bottlenecks are smoothed out; waste is kept to a minimum. The process capitalizes on the full potential of existing technology; and the cycle time is reduced to a minimum.

Efficiency indicators are identified and performance is reviewed against these. For your customer, increasing efficiency is likely to result in reductions in costs, and quicker response times.

ACTIVITY 8

Do your processes deliver the output in the most efficient manner? How do you know?

RESPONSIVE

A responsive process more readily **accommodates changes**. We operate in turbulent times. External changes in the marketplace, in the social, economic, political and legal environments are wide ranging and relentless. Developments in technology, and radical changes in competitive products or services may render your output – or your process – obsolete.

So excellent processes incorporate environmental scans to stay in touch with latest developments, and proactively to anticipate action required. But they don't just do the scans – they do something about them. Findings are incorporated into reviews and changes are implemented to improve the process.

ACTIVITY 9

What changes have been made to your processes recently? Why were they made?

Process change	Reason for change

People

Processes cannot achieve anything on their own: people operate the processes. So managing the process means managing the people. However this is no simple task.

On the one hand, each individual probably knows more about their own part of the process than anyone else; they operate it from day to day. So you need to access and build on that knowledge and expertise. On the other hand, because identity is often strongly invested in work, changing what people do may trigger complex emotional reactions and undermine commitment and motivation.

At the same time, as we have already mentioned in Section 1, most process practitioners have also emphasized a structural element to the people dimension. If you want people to share an understanding of and a commitment to the process, you have to create opportunities for them to do so.

LEADERSHIP

Excellent processes have someone – a process owner – who takes personal responsibility for the process and enables its success. The process owner sets up the structural opportunities for stakeholders – forms the process improvement team, facilitates the learning, supports the efforts. He or she secures the resources, funding and time allocation, and mediates between the process improvement team and the rest of the organization, or external contacts. The process owner holds the vision of where the process is going and co-ordinates the efforts of all stakeholders to ensure it achieves its objectives and stays on target.

CAPABILITY

The traditional functional hierarchy may make it difficult to communicate across functional divides. If you want people to work together on a process, you need a set-up that facilitates and rewards collaboration rather than individual allegiances and internal politicking.

People need to know their own roles and responsibilities, and how these fit into the bigger picture. They need to share information and a common understanding of the process as a whole. They need the skills and knowledge to achieve what is expected of them. It must matter to them personally whether the process achieves its goals. Finally, they must operate effectively as a team, to optimize their strengths and minimize the impact of individual weaknesses.

ACTIVITY 10

What do you feel are the main people issues for your processes? Why?

Issue	Reason

FEEDBACK

A more detailed analysis of these issues is set out in Section 6.

The systems

The systems are the 'hidden' elements of process excellence. Improving people's skills or streamlining the process itself are immediately visible and deliver immediate returns. Systems may seem like burdensome bureaucracy. However, there is no point trying to improve a chaotic process; until the process is defined and stabilized, you have no way of knowing if the results you get are created by what you do, or by chance. Which means that improving the process may become a frustrating business.

DEFINITION

Excellent processes are consistent, not chaotic or random. The causal links and inter-dependencies with other processes have been clarified and managed. The processes are formalized and documented in detail, along with the outputs at every stage. Key measures are known and specified, and the paperwork truly reflects what happens on the ground. It's not a question of a process that looks wonderful on paper, but which is inoperable in practice.

ACTIVITY 11

How far does the reality match the documentation in your processes? Where do discrepancies creep in?

REVIEW

Even a process that was once world class will lose its edge over time; your competitors will be moving forward, even if you don't. So excellent processes stay excellent by setting and reviewing performance against relevant indicators. There should be a system for such reviews on a regular basis, so that reviews are an automatic element in the process. Reviews also ensure that action is taken where necessary to adjust and improve the process.

ACTIVITY 12

When was the last formal review of your process? Who was involved? What action was taken as a result of findings?

Date of review

People involved

Findings	**Action**

The process scorecard

If you have done the activities above, you have already begun to think about how your processes are performing. The process scorecard shown in Figure 10 is a handy tool to help you formalize your evaluation.

ACTIVITY 13   A4

Use the process scorecard to evaluate one of your processes. For each criterion, circle the description that most closely matches the process **as it is now**. Transfer the score to the column on the right-hand side, and then total your score for each process. This is your current **process capability** score. Now subtract this score from 28 (the maximum). This is the process's **potential for improvement**.

Criterion	0	1	2	3	4	Score
Effectiveness	Output requirements have not been identified for this process	Output requirements assumed (rather than verified) for all process customers	Output requirements verified with all process customers, sometimes achieved	Outputs to each process customer meet requirements most of the time	Outputs to all process customers consistently meet requirements every time	
Efficiency	Efficiency indicators not identified	Efficiency indicators agreed	Efficiency measures taken routinely and used for setting improvement targets	Efficiency being continuously improved	Proven world-class levels of efficiency being achieved	
Responsiveness	There is no regular scan of external or internal environment to monitor changes that may affect the process	Scans are conducted and the information is fed into the process on a regular basis	Scans have been used to identify opportunities for improvement (including technology)	Some opportunities identified by the scan have been implemented	All opportunities identified have been optimized (i.e. time and effort invested in proportion to the expected gain)	
Leadership	No one owns this process	Process owner appointed	Owner has fully accepted responsibilities and understands all process tools and techniques	The success of this process impacts on the process owner's personal awards. Owner skilled with process tools, effective leader	Process owner is recognized as a role model. Has been rewarded for improvements	
Capability	Those involved do not understand the whole process	Those involved understand the process	All involved know their own responsibilities and are competent	All highly competent and committed, work as a team. They know each others' responsibilities in outline, are rewarded for the success of this process	Recognized role models, working with process customers and suppliers to improve the process	
Definition	Achieving the output is almost haphazard or incidental. The process exists, but has not been documented.	The transformations, inputs and outputs have all been agreed, documented and accurately flowcharted	Measurement mechanisms included in process definition	Audits show process and documents match	The process is consistent, proven, and full understood	
Review	No system of regular reviews; or else, reactive and ad hoc reviews only	Review programme set up, with specific review objectives	Systematic review plan is being followed, including feedback and corrective action	Systematic review plan is leading to improvements via joint improvement teams	All involved in systematic plan and review. Reviews have led to significant improvements	
					GRAND TOTAL:	

Figure 10 Process scorecard (abridged and adapted from Tucker, 1996, p.14)

FEEDBACK

How did you do? The maximum process capability score on the scorecard for excellent processes is 28. Longer established processes in particular may end up with mainly 1s or 0s, and a grand total of 7 would not be unusual. Poor scores may seem shocking at first (and they are certainly no cause for complacency) but don't forget that they indicate enormous potential for improvement. So you will find plenty of opportunity to develop your process management skills. And after all, that's why you're working through this workbook.

Which processes?

The scorecard is a handy health check for your processes, and reveals where they may be lacking. Managing and improving the three dimensions (process, people, systems) of quality can be a lot of work and you may be responsible for several different processes. How do you know where to focus your attention?

Processes exist to deliver outputs for your customers, or to achieve the organization's objectives. Your critical processes are therefore the processes that contribute most to the outputs for customers or the organizational objectives. The better you manage these, the greater the likelihood that you will secure and retain customers (or public co-operation and support); and the greater the organizational gain.

ADDING VALUE FOR THE CUSTOMER

A process takes inputs, works on them, and delivers an output that your customers want: it **adds value.** Value in this case is determined by the customer. For example, a manufacturing process takes various raw materials or components (inputs), and assembles them to transform them into the finished product or output – a washing machine, say. A complete washing machine is worth more than a box of bits to most customers, so the process has added value.

Not all activities add value in the customers' eyes. For example, special colours or finishes may be highly valued in cars, and customers may be prepared to pay more for, say, black or metallic finishes. But when it comes to hardback books, the average customer is unlikely to care whether the binding is red or black under the dustjacket – even if one option costs you more or takes you longer.

CASE STUDY

A software company had always used the priority 9 a.m. service to deliver its products to customers; this was around twice as expensive as the standard 12 noon delivery. However, support staff noticed that customers rarely called for help on installation until later in the day, or even the following day. A brief telephone survey revealed that customers would be just as happy with a 12 noon delivery – there were usually other priorities early in the day. So the company changed to the later delivery and saved over £20 000 a year, which it was able to pass on to delighted customers.

ACTIVITY 14

Go back to the processes you identified in Activity 1. If you stopped any of these processes, how would your external customer be affected?

Process   **Effect on external customer**

Which would have the greatest effect on the customer?

Are there any that would have no effect on the customer? If so, why do you continue to do them?

ACHIEVING THE ORGANIZATION'S OBJECTIVES

A process may also take inputs and work on them to deliver outputs that enable the organization to achieve its objectives. These may include creating and sustaining the organization's values and culture; devising and implementing policies and strategies that enable the organization to attract employees, suppliers and customers or to optimize the potential for gains; or any of the support processes such as recruitment or training which develop the inherent capability of the organization.

ACTIVITY 15

Take a look at your organization's mission (or vision) statement, and the organizational objectives. (These are commonly published in the Annual Report, or in internal publicity, at the start of each year. If your organization doesn't publish them, use your own departmental or team objectives, which may be set at your annual appraisal.) Which of your processes identified in Activity 1 contribute to these objectives – and what do they contribute?

Mission statement

Process   **Contribution**

A WASTE OF TIME?

Recent research indicates that activities adding no value to either the customer or the organization may account for as much as 60 per cent of organizational effort. This 60 per cent is deadweight cost, reducing your productivity.

If a process is not adding value to one or more of the business stakeholders, then it is simply consuming resources (time, effort, energy, people, etc.) that should be focused elsewhere.

(Tucker, 1996)

Weighing up the choice

When you begin process management efforts, it may be tempting to 'start small'. You want time to try out the tools and techniques, and get to grips with the issues of process improvement. But clearly, the potential for gain is greatest where the impact on the customer or the organization is greatest. While improving the process for claiming expenses might bring you some benefits, you may have much more to gain from critical processes such as setting team objectives, or building your customer base.

ACTIVITY 16

Take your list of processes identified in Section 1 and write them down in Column 1 of the table below.

1   Calculate the potential for improvement (P) of each process, (28 – score on scorecard = P) and write this in the second column.
2   Now award points according to their impact on the customer or organizational objectives (I), so that the process with greatest impact has the highest score, and the one with least impact scores 1.
3   Multiply the two scores; the highest total indicates where gain may be greatest. Select the top priority process on which you will focus your improvement efforts.

Process	Potential for improvement (P)	Impact (I) on customers/ organization	P x I = Total

Summary

Three factors determine how far the process delivers what the customers want and need; and its contribution to the organizational objectives:

- the process itself
- the people who operate it
- the systems that support it

The process must be:

- effective (the output must be what customers want)
- efficient (process creates the output using the least resources)
- responsive (process changes to reflect changes in the external environment, competition, etc.)

A process owner should take personal responsibility for the process and its success. Process operators need:

- information
- skills and knowledge
- resources and supports
- incentives, personal ownership and motivation

Once the process has been systematized and documented, the next step is to ensure that it is regularly and proactively reviewed, and that any action required as a result is promptly implemented.

Critical processes are those processes that have the greatest impact on the organization's objectives or on the customer. Processes that have both greatest potential for improvement and greatest impact on the customer or organizational objectives, are therefore the priorities for any improvement efforts.

Section 3 Process mapping

In this section of the workbook, we consider the significance of documenting the process, and recommend the involvement of stakeholders at an early stage. We introduce the techniques of process mapping (or flowcharting), and explore the different perspectives offered by different types of flowchart. Finally, we offer guidelines on involving stakeholders in process mapping efforts.

When you have worked through this section of the workbook, you will be able to:

- recognize the benefits of involving stakeholders in process improvement
- document existing processes using process mapping techniques
- select the type of diagram most appropriate to your needs

The whole process

To manage a process, you must first understand how it works. You may find when you start thinking about processes that no-one knows the whole story, or that it's difficult to get a picture of how it all fits together. Although processes are the way the organization meets customer wants and needs, and achieves its objectives (and are therefore of central importance to the organization) they span multiple dimensions:

- inputs (information, materials, ideas, etc. – including customer wants and needs)
- the activities or transformations (some of which may be processes or subprocesses in their own right)
- the people who do them (and the different functions to which they belong)
- the resources required to do them
- the time it takes to do them
- the order in which they are done
- where they are done
- the intermediate outputs at every stage (delivered to internal customers)
- the eventual output (delivered to the external customer)

People may only know the details of their own 'bit', but the effectiveness, efficiency and responsiveness of a process depend on co-ordinating all these bits and optimizing the process as a whole.

In many organizations, there are many individual groups all doing a good job. They are doing their own thing, very interested in meeting or beating their measurements, but not understanding or caring about how their activities affect others further down the line.

(Harrington, 1991, p.15)

It's no good improving individual activities without considering their impact on the rest of the process.

CASE STUDY

Imagine a biscuit factory increasing production without matching increases in packing capability. As the biscuits rolled off the production line, they would begin to stack up; the pressure on packers would increase. They'd probably be able to put in a special effort for a while, so they'd be sending more packs down the line. But sooner or later, the sheer volume produced might mean that unpacked biscuits would start to spill out over the hoppers and onto the floor. Product would be wasted. Packers would begin to get upset. They might slow down or even stop work altogether.

ACTIVITY 17

Thinking back to one of the critical processes you identified in Activity 15, what gaps can you identify in your knowledge of any of the factors in the checklist on page 32? Who has the information you need?

Who knows, who cares, who can?

Each person involved in the process – from the supplier through every member of staff to the eventual customer – has a stake in it. Each probably knows their own element better than anyone else. If someone's been preparing and archiving microfiche records for the last six years, they have inside knowledge about that part of the records process which may be invaluable when you want to improve it. So it makes sense to harness their experience and seek their ideas for improving the system.

CASE STUDY

James Champy (1995, p.93) tells the story of how some managers at Xerox learned this particular lesson the hard – and public – way. One of their copiers, the 3300, was proving unreliable. At the annual shareholders' meeting, an assembly line worker got up and said: 'We all knew the 3300 was a piece of junk. We could have told you. Why didn't you ask us?'. Production was immediately suspended and a team of stakeholders including assembly line workers began work to resolve the problems.

VESTED INTERESTS

Work may be a defining factor in how individuals see themselves, and in their sense of self-worth. Any changes may trigger powerful and often unconscious emotional reactions – such as suspicion, fear, resentment – which may block or seriously undermine any improvement efforts. The more you are able to involve people in improvement efforts that affect their work, the more likely they are to feel a sense of ownership, and approach any changes in a more positive way: with high hopes, energy and enthusiasm.

ACTIVITY 18

How do you think the people you identified in Activity 17 might feel about any changes to the process you have selected for improvement?

What are their priorities likely to be?

What do you think they each stand to gain?

BUILDING OWNERSHIP

One way you can build commitment to any changes is to get stakeholders involved in process improvement efforts from the start. This gives them a chance to work things out and recognize for themselves the need to change, so that resistance is minimized. It enables you to tap into their ideas early enough to be able to use them, and this not only builds ownership, it is likely to improve the quality of any changes you may make.

Operating a process that is ineffective, inefficient, or too rigid to meet customer needs can be a frustrating and undermining experience. People want to feel pride in what they do, to make a contribution. So involving people in improvement efforts can also increase personal job satisfaction, the quality of teamworking, and raise staff morale. By the same token, however, seeking their ideas and then ignoring them is likely to generate considerable bad feeling and disillusion.

AN OPPORTUNITY TO COLLABORATE

This workbook is about developing your own skills and understanding. But the framework for process improvement and the tools and techniques that go with it may be equally relevant for your team. Sharing them with your team may offer the opportunity for productive collaboration and consolidate your own learning.

You may wish to try out on your own the tools and techniques for learning purposes. Then, once you're comfortable with them, one of the best ways to begin understanding processes is to meet with the process stakeholders and pool your knowledge by documenting the process.

Putting it on paper

Given the complexities of processes, one of the easiest ways to get to grips with them is to draw them. Diagrams are compact; they simplify access; and they are precise. They are also pretty universal (once you are familiar with the conventions, what the different symbols mean, and so on). Take the electronic circuit diagram for a computer, or an architectural floorplan, for example. Each may be drawn on a single page. But just imagine how complicated it would be to communicate the same information in words – or to wade through those words to find the information you needed to solder a single connection or install the plumbing.

You can illustrate how a process works in flowcharts, also known as **process maps**. Process maps don't require any special drawing skills and only a minimum of special symbols. But they do help you to get an overview of the whole process, and how the different activities fit together. In fact, you've already encountered some simple process maps in Section 1 – Figures 2 and 4 that showed a diagram booking your holiday; or picking, wrapping and despatching goods, for example.

CHECKING IT OUT

Once you've got the diagram in front of you, everyone will be working from the same information. You will be able to check out the order, the connections, the inputs and outputs at every stage, and who is responsible for them. The key questions for process management come into their own here:

- why are we doing this at all?
- why are we doing it in this particular way?
- is there a better way to do it?

Process maps are also acceptable to BSI and other ISO9000 accrediting organizations for describing the production, installation and servicing process that directly affects quality (see ISO9000 paragraph 4.9, Process control).

There are various different types of flowchart or process map, depending on what kinds of details you want to show, and who the chart is for.

A simple start (flowcharts)

A simple flowchart illustrates the main activities and the order in which they must be done. Activities are represented by rectangles and the direction of the process flow by arrows.

First, decide which process you're going to work on, then brainstorm all the activities involved. Start each activity with a verb or 'doing' word (such as 'choose', 'list', 'file' or 'repair'). Keep them as short and simple as possible. Arrange these activities into the order in which they occur. Then draw the diagram, as large as you can; write each activity in a separate box, with arrows between the boxes to show the direction of flow. Flowcharts are usually organized so that the flow moves left to right, or top to bottom.

To illustrate, the flowchart for the process of 'drawing a flowchart' might look something like Figure 11.

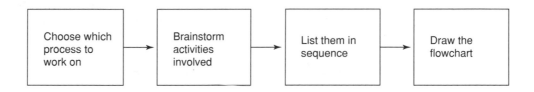

Figure 11   A simple flowchart

PROS AND CONS

On the plus side, this is a very simple and accessible way to present the information; even newcomers to the process should be able to grasp the essence of it. But it doesn't tell you who does the activities, or where, and it doesn't show the outputs or the inputs you need to achieve them.

ACTIVITY 19

Choose a simple process with which you are familiar and draw it using flowchart techniques.

Adding the frills (integrated flowcharts)

Once you've got the basic shape, you can add in any information you need about inputs and outputs at various stages.

Don't draw this information in boxes like the activities – you'll need to distinguish them in some way. Write them in open brackets (as shown in Figure 12) or use a letter code and give details in the key. If you are drawing your chart top to bottom, set your inputs to the left, and specify the intermediate outputs (those that become the inputs for the next activity) on the arrows of the main flow. The result might look something like that shown in Figure 12.

In Figure 12, we have ignored any outputs that are not required later in the process. However, these can be included on the right-hand side of the central flowchart, using an open bracket or code letter, as for the inputs.

PROS AND CONS

The flowchart is still quite clear, and you have included inputs and outputs, which are quantifiable, and which therefore may be compared against specifications or standards to monitor how you're doing and where any problems creep in. But you still haven't made it clear who does what, or where.

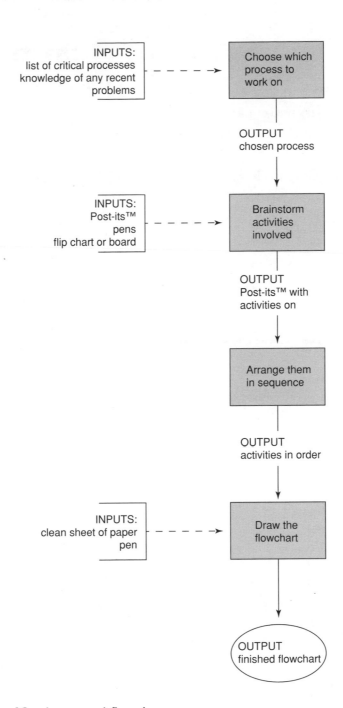

Figure 12   Integrated flowchart

ACTIVITY 20

Take the flowchart you prepared for Activity 19, and add in the inputs and outputs where appropriate.

Buttons and bows (layout flowcharts)

If **where** things happen is important – for example, if you're reviewing a particularly complex documentation process, where you need to track its path through the organization – then a **layout** flowchart may be what you need.

Here, the flowchart is superimposed onto a plan of the location. (You could equally well use a map, or a symbolic representation of diverse sites. Scale doesn't really matter, although it would be useful to have some indication of the relative distance of each activity from the next.) The activities are drawn in where they happen, and arrows join each to the next – wherever that might be. For example, a layout flowchart for sending out an invoice might look something like that shown in Figure 13.

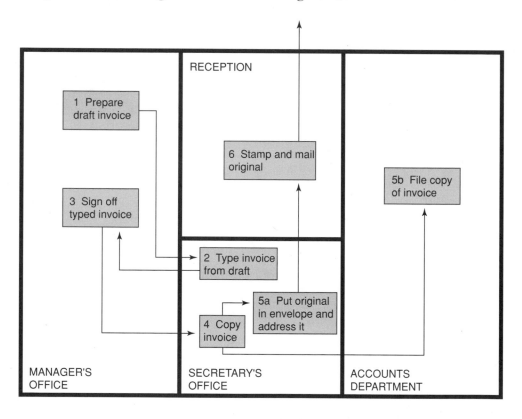

Figure 13   Layout flowchart

Figure 13 shows the floorplan of one part of the organization, with the manager's office on the left, the secretary next to him/her, and the accounts department on the far right. The manager prepares a draft invoice, which the secretary types up. Once it is approved, the secretary copies it, envelopes the original, and sends the copy to accounts, who then file it. Reception sends out the enveloped original. Each of the activities is numbered for ease of reference, and the direction of flow is indicated by the arrows. Notice that there are two outputs from activity 4 – the copy and the original, which each then follow separate paths.

PROS AND CONS

This technique may have echoes of Cluedo, but it can make a powerful point. It helps to highlight where work is being returned, or where transfers between departments or individuals may cause delay, or where the layout itself causes delay because the outputs have to travel further than they need.

ACTIVITY 21

Take a few moments to try the layout technique with a simple process with which you are familiar. Pick something that involves transferring the intermediate outputs from one location to another.

Bells... (deployment flowcharts)

If you need to get to grips with roles and responsibilities – who does what (and possibly when) – then a **deployment** flowchart is what you need. The page is divided into columns, representing each individual or group involved in the process. The activities are drawn in, sequentially as for a simple flow-chart; but this time, each activity appears underneath the name of the person who does it. You'll end up with something like Figure 14.

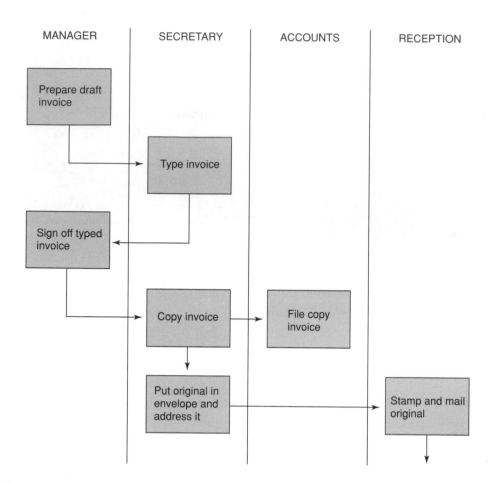

Figure 14   Deployment flowchart

PROS AND CONS

This kind of chart is relatively compact, and the columns make it easier to read than the layout flowchart. But it puts the spotlight on the handovers between individuals. Especially when used with some of the symbols (see below) it can reveal where problems or delays creep in. You can add timings down the left-hand side, to begin to quantify any delays, if that would be useful. Outputs can be included, and there are therefore obvious stages within the process where you can compare these against specifications, to check that the process is on target.

ACTIVITY 22

Redraw the simple process from your layout chart, as a deployment chart.

How does this change the information you can gain about the process?

... And whistles (extra symbols)

It may help to use different symbols to differentiate various kinds of activity or transfer. There are a number of conventions: it makes little difference which you use, so long as you are consistent and the people who use the chart understand them. Figure 15 gives one version of some common symbols, and what they mean.

If the process is complex – or if there are subprocesses involved, which need to be documented in their own right – you may not be able to fit everything on the same diagram. When you get to the edge of the page (or the relevant subprocess), use an output connector symbol, and continue on a separate diagram, starting with an input connector showing the same letter code.

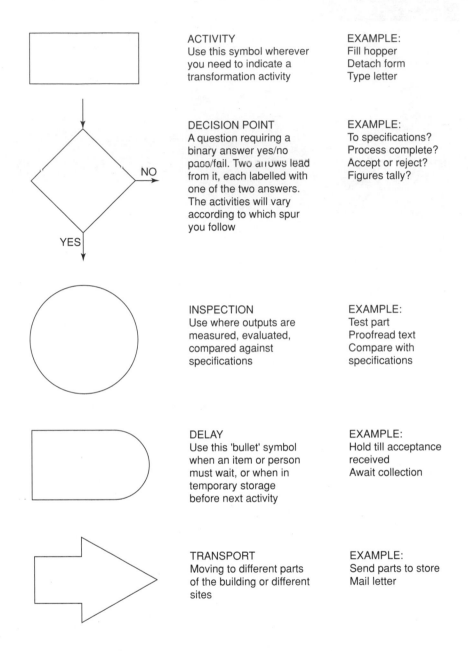

ACTIVITY
Use this symbol wherever you need to indicate a transformation activity

EXAMPLE:
Fill hopper
Detach form
Type letter

DECISION POINT
A question requiring a binary answer yes/no pass/fail. Two arrows lead from it, each labelled with one of the two answers. The activities will vary according to which spur you follow

EXAMPLE:
To specifications?
Process complete?
Accept or reject?
Figures tally?

INSPECTION
Use where outputs are measured, evaluated, compared against specifications

EXAMPLE:
Test part
Proofread text
Compare with specifications

DELAY
Use this 'bullet' symbol when an item or person must wait, or when in temporary storage before next activity

EXAMPLE:
Hold till acceptance received
Await collection

TRANSPORT
Moving to different parts of the building or different sites

EXAMPLE:
Send parts to store
Mail letter

Figure 15   Some symbols for process maps (abridged and adapted from Harrington, 1991, pp.96-98)

ACTIVITY 23

Which of these three types of flowchart will be most appropriate to document the critical processes you selected for improvement efforts in Section 2? Bear in mind the audience for the flowchart – who will contribute to it, who will use it, and how they will use it.

	Process
Integrated	
Layout	
Deployment	

A snapshot of your process

Once you are comfortable with the flowchart options and what the symbols mean, you are ready to start drawing your chosen critical process as it is right now. This is a kind of snapshot of how it is actually operating (rather than how you or others would like it to work, or how it is supposed to work).

The process map is best created by a group or team, with representatives of all stakeholders and all stages of the process (up to a maximum of about eight: beyond that, the meeting can get cumbersome – not to mention noisy!) Choose your members carefully and aim for a balanced team. Include sceptics, as well as those who are keen to try new techniques – they'll keep each other on their toes. Too heavy on the enthusiasts, and the risk is that vital implementation issues may be ignored. Too heavy on the sceptics, and you may find that you get bogged down, or that goals and objectives are not challenging enough.

GETTING DOWN TO IT

For these sessions, it's best to book a meeting room and get away from the usual work environment (perhaps even off site), so that you're not interrupted by phone calls or visitors. Give yourselves plenty of time – you'll have to judge this for yourself, but two hours might be the minimum for a relatively simple process that has not been documented before. You'll need Post-its™, pens, and a board or flipchart pad.

Start off by agreeing where the process ends – the final output to your internal or external customer – and where it begins. Then decide what kind of flowchart you're going to prepare, depending on the purpose of your chart, and the audience. Brainstorm the activities involved, and write each on a separate Post-it™. (Remember that this exercise is about documenting the process as it currently operates – not what is supposed to happen: we'll come to that later.)

Stick the activity Post-its™, in the order in which they happen, on the board or flipchart (or wall – processes have a habit of spreading). When you all agree that the order and layout accurately represents your process, transfer it onto paper. Draw your finished diagram as large as reasonably possible, for ease of reference. As we suggested above, if your process is particularly large or complex, you may find it helpful to designate subprocesses with output connector symbols, then draw them separately. Figure 16 illustrates the process of creating a flowchart.

RELEASING THE ENERGY

This exercise is a real energizer: you may be amazed how lightbulbs suddenly go on in people's heads, as they see the whole picture, realize the whys and wherefores, and how their activities contribute to the output. Discussions may grow quite heated as you arrange the Post-its™ and the flowchart emerges. People are talking about something in which they have a stake, so they may feel vulnerable, angry, defensive, even passionate. Try to focus on the actual activities, rather than the individuals concerned; it's not a question of blame or fault.

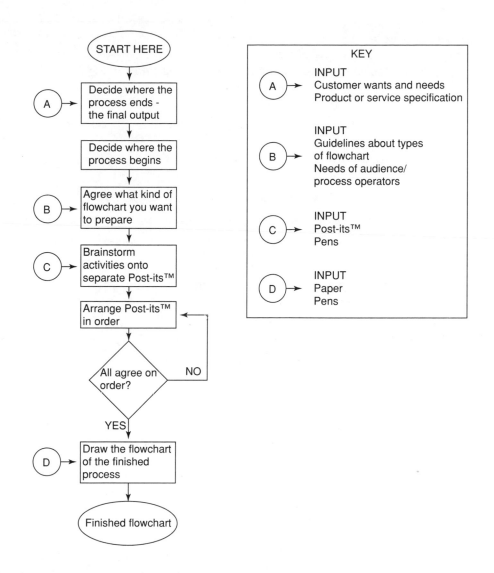

Figure 16 Creating your flowchart

ACTIVITY 24

You've had the theory; now it's a question of doing it.
EITHER

- if you feel ready to tackle it, get together with your team to diagram your critical process
  OR

- try to draw your critical process on your own, and then make some time to go through it with someone who is involved in the process. How far does your diagram reflect their understanding of the process? Ask them to question you on any point that isn't clear, and adjust your process map accordingly, so that it is clear enough for even a novice to read and use.

Summary

If you want to manage something, you must first understand it. It's vital to develop a holistic understanding of your business process, and the context in which it operates, before you can begin to manage or improve its outputs. People often know only their own 'bits', so it is a question of combining the knowledge and perspectives of all stakeholders.

Process maps or **flowcharts** are one of the most effective tools to develop and share understanding of the process as a whole, its inputs and outputs, who does what, where and when. They may help to reveal inefficiencies and waste, duplication and gaps.

The simple flowchart diagrams the main activities and the order in which they are done. Inputs and outputs may be added, and special flowchart symbols used to signify different types of activity or other elements of the process. **Layout flowcharts** use maps or floorplans to illustrate where activities occur, and the journey that internal or intermediate outputs must take to create the eventual output for customers. **Deployment flowcharts** reveal individual responsibility and handover points.

Once you have selected your critical process, the next step is to diagram your process **as it is now** rather than how you would like it to be, or how it is supposed to be. Doing this with your team can help to build team energy and enthusiasm, and develop ownership and commitment to any changes.

Section 4 Identifying process improvements

In this section of the workbook, we focus on the process itself and consider what the process mapping exercise has revealed about the efficiency of the process. Some quick wins may be possible by eliminating non value-adding steps, parallel processing, altering the layout, or generally smoothing the path of the process. Fishbone diagrams may help to reveal the root cause of repeat errors so that action can be taken. We explore the continuum from incremental improvement to existing processes, through to clean slate re-engineering.

When you have worked through this section of the workbook, you will be able to:

- use the process map to identify opportunities for streamlining
- use fishbone cause-and-effect diagrams to identify the causes of problems
- consider more radical approaches to design the process from the customer out

What next?

Having documented the process as it now operates, the next step is to identify where any problems, inadequacies or potential for improvement occur in the process – whether inherent in the process itself (including its outputs), in the people who operate it, or in the systems that support it. Then you can generate ideas for correcting them. Finally, when you've generated your ideas, you can evaluate them, weigh up the implications, and decide which you want to pursue (see Section 7).

The phase of generating improvements may be quite a lengthy business: you'll be gathering information on several different fronts, and feeding it back to the team. For the sake of clarity in this workbook, we've separated out process, system and people improvements, and approached them sequentially. However, the likelihood is that you'll be investigating them in parallel; and you'll need to consider all the options before you decide which you're going to implement.

Streamlining

Putting together the process diagram often releases quite an impetus for action: people want to get on and do something NOW. Indeed, the diagram may have revealed some immediate opportunities for improving the process. These are likely to be ways of doing the same thing, better: more efficiently, using fewer resources, or more quickly. Harrington (1991) refers to these types of solutions as **streamlining**.

QUICK WINS

You may have spotted opportunities to:

- **eliminate duplication** (e.g. both personnel and the manager keeping separate paper-based records on employees)
- **eliminate redundant** steps (and especially bureaucratic paperwork) which add no value for the organization or the customer (e.g. keeping paper-based records as well as computer-based records)
- **smooth the process** by reducing handovers or transportation to different sites
- **improve the layout** through which the outputs must flow, so as to reduce the distance between sequential activities
- **simplify the process** by reducing the number of steps
- **process in parallel** (where different people or areas complete different activities at the same time, rather than sequentially – see also Process cycle time, page 56)
- **automate or computerize** any part of the process

You may be surprised just what comes up:

Some of the changes seemed obvious in hindsight, but they're the kinds of things you overlook in the day to day stresses of running a business. When you step back and pull the whole process apart, suddenly they leap out at you.
   (Ron Rittenmeyer, Frito-Lay Business Systems, quoted in Champy, 1995, p.136)

These quick wins are not to be sneezed at: some of them may produce very substantial benefits for the organization. Before pursuing any of your ideas, you'll need a chance to see how they fit in with other improvements that may be required. However, people may feel they're still 'on the agenda' until you deal with them, so it's worth making a point of brainstorming ideas for quick wins and listing them for later consideration.

ACTIVITY 25

What opportunities can you immediately see in your process map (Activity 24) for quick wins? Make a note of these: we'll be evaluating them in Section 7.

ERROR-PROOFING

If you wanted to do everything wrong in your process, what would you do? Error-proofing involves brainstorming possible sources of error or problems, and then making it difficult to make these mistakes.

For example, window envelopes may prevent snarl-ups on the printer, or letters being sent to the wrong people. Having the photocopier automatically return to standard single copies after a short delay means people are less likely to end up with multiple copies or magnification they don't want, simply because they didn't check before copying. If the task is complex, what about breaking it down into smaller chunks, or providing some kind of job aid to help get it right?

ACTIVITY 26

What opportunities can you see for error-proofing your process? Make a note of your ideas. We'll return to evaluate them in Section 7.

CRITICAL EXAMINATION

The critical examination matrix (Figure 17) offers a more structured approach to challenge every activity on the process map – including delays, transportation and storage. This can be quite time consuming, but because it is so thorough and systematic, it will ensure that you don't miss any possibilities.

WHAT is done?	WHY is it done?	What ELSE could be done?	What else SHOULD be done?
HOW is it done?	WHY that way?	How ELSE could it be done?	How else SHOULD it be done?
WHEN is it done?	WHY then?	When ELSE could it be done?	When else SHOULD it be done?
WHERE is it done?	WHY there?	Where ELSE could it be done?	Where else SHOULD it be done?
WHO does it?	WHY them?	Who ELSE could do it?	Who else SHOULD do it?

Figure 17   Critical examination matrix

ACTIVITY 27

Use the first three columns of the critical examination matrix (Figure 17 and below) to challenge every step of your process. What possibilities does this reveal for improvement? We'll move on to evaluate these and decide what you should do later.

WHAT is done?	WHY is it done?	What ELSE could be done?
HOW is it done?	WHY that way?	How ELSE could it be done?
WHEN is it done?	WHY then?	When ELSE could it be done?
WHERE is it done?	WHY there?	Where ELSE could it be done?
WHO does it?	WHY them?	Who ELSE could do it?

More challenging possibilities

The quick wins and critical examination techniques outlined above are likely to generate ideas based on the existing process. But two other techniques may help to generate more innovative and challenging possibilities.

FISHBONE DIAGRAM

*The vast majority of problems occur over and over again because the **root cause** is not established or eradicated.*

(Fowler and Graves, 1995, p.75)

For more complex errors – or problems that have cropped up repeatedly – the **fishbone** or cause-and-effect diagram may help you get to the bottom of what's actually going on. It may be useful, for example, in working out the root causes of:

- **rework and returns** where a proportion of outputs are regularly returned to an earlier stage because they aren't up to standard
- **delays** where an output ends up waiting or not being worked on for any period
- **long cycle times** (from start to finish of the process)

The fishbone diagram is a brainstorming technique that's probably best conducted with the team, to get several different perspectives on the problem.

Use as large a board or piece of paper as you can. Draw a 'fish skeleton' right across the page, with a head, a backbone, and four or six main bones branching off it.

Write your problem or error in the fish head. Label the main bones with the main factors you see as contributing to the problem. Alternatively use the standard 'PEM/PEM' prompts, as shown in Figure 18: People–Environment–Methods; Plant–Equipment–Materials (or the 4M prompts: Men, Materials, Methods, Machinery). Your diagram should look something like Figure 18 before you start brainstorming ideas.

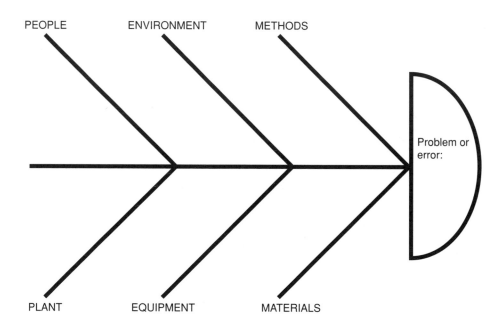

Figure 18   Fishbone diagram

Next, brainstorm ideas as to the causes of the problem and write each up on a smaller bone feeding into the appropriate main bone. (It may be easiest to write them onto Post-its™ first, so that you can move them around and alter the order.) Your diagram might end up looking something like Figure 19.

Pursue each cause to the limit – keep asking WHY? Why are people the problem? Because they are untrained. Why are people untrained? Because people are too busy to train them. Why are people overloaded? Because they're covering for absent staff (and so on).

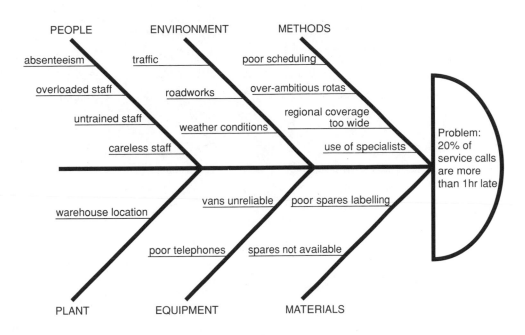

Figure 19 Updated fisbone diagram

Take one error or problem that has occurred repeatedly, and do a fishbone diagram to uncover the root causes. Once more, make a note of any ideas this triggers for improving the situation. We'll return to these in Section 7.

PROCESS CYCLE TIME

There may also be considerable gains from improving the cycle time – the total length of time it takes for the process to run from start to finish. The cycle time is usually considerably longer than the time for each of the individual activities added together. Take a look at this simplified example of a memo-writing process to see how:

Activity	Activity time (hours)	Cycle time (hours)
Manager writes memo	0.2 hours	0.2 hours
Secretary collects mail for typing (twice a day, average delay 12 hours)	0.1 hours	12 hours
DELAY: secretary is busy, can't type immediately. Average waiting time 26 hours		26 hours
Secretary types memo and sends for signature	0.3 hours	0.3 hours
Manager signs memo (twice a day) and returns for mailing 5 p.m.	0.1 hours	12 hours
Secretary collects memo 9 a.m.	0.1 hours	16 hours
DELAY waiting for next trip to copier		5 hours
Secretary copies memo, addresses envelopes	0.3 hours	0.3 hours
Secretary takes memo to mail at 5 p.m.	0.1 hours	2.7 hours
TOTALS	1.2 hours	74.5 hours

(Adapted from Harrington, 1991, p.126)

While the activities themselves only took a total of 1.2 hours (1 hour 12 minutes), the total cycle time – the time it actually took to deliver the output – was more than three days.

Cycle time is what your customer sees, whether it's the time:

- from sending off the mail order form, to receiving the goods
- from arriving at casualty department with a broken wrist, to leaving with a plaster cast
- from paying in the deposit, to the date it is credited in the bank

Reducing the length of time taken to complete each individual activity may not benefit the customer if it doesn't lead to reductions in the cycle time. Reducing the cycle time can make a dramatic difference for the customer. Harrington (1991, p.105) cites the example of IBM who reduced cycle time by 30 per cent in one area – and gained themselves a 300 per cent increase in sales.

Different outputs?

However, all these improvement efforts may be in vain if the process doesn't deliver the outputs that customers want in the first place. If the output is wrong, customers will still be dissatisfied even if you deliver it more quickly or more pleasantly, or whatever. So the key question is: does the process deliver the outputs that customers actually want at every stage? This, of course, is the prime indicator of effectiveness, highlighted in the process scorecard in Section 2.

Your output to customers is much more than the product or service the organization is nominally providing:

Customers ... expect every interface to be a pleasure. They expect the salesperson to be friendly and knowledgeable, the salesroom clean and pleasant, the bills readable and accurate, the package attractive and easy to open, the service people responsive and competent, the phones answered on the second ring and not to be put on hold.

(Harrington, 1991, p.5)

CUSTOMER EXPECTATIONS

Customers buy into the whole package, which includes:

- the product or service itself (Is this formally specified? What leeway or tolerance is there in this specification?)
- the cost
- the people who deliver it (how they look, the way they dress, speak, behave, and treat the customer)
- the phone, email, or other, computerized contacts – how long will it take to respond?
- the paperwork
- the surroundings in which the product or service is delivered
- the follow-ups – including what you will do if anything does go wrong
- how long the transaction takes
- the cycle time from order or service request through to delivery
- how long the product or service lasts

For example, expectations of the police force might include not chewing gum or smoking while dealing with members of the public; keeping to the speed limit (except when on emergency); answering phone calls by the fourth ring; despatching assistance to emergency calls within ten minutes of call received.

Internal customers have similar kinds of expectations. Consider a report that your manager wants from you on some key aspect of your work. He or she is likely to have specified the purpose, the scope, the delivery date;

but there may also be implicit expectations about the size and colour of paper you use, the font and format in which the text is drafted, the number of copies you supply.

These expectations should inform and shape the process:

A correctly-designed business process has the voice and perspective of the customer 'built in'.

(Davenport, 1993, p.15)

Champy suggests:

Define your standards and objectives from your customer's point of view. They'll be impossibly ambitious as a result, but in striving to meet them you may well achieve the 'impossible'.

(Champy, 1995, p.137)

ACTIVITY 29

What standards does your customer expect from your process? Take some time to run through the checklist on page 57, and try to specify them in as much detail as you can.

How 'reasonable' are these expectations?

Have you actually agreed these together (or is it just a wishlist on their part, or a guess on yours)?

If not, how could you bring them to the table for negotiation?

How could you set these kinds of standards for your suppliers?

You have already evaluated the effectiveness of the output itself (in Section 2), but you may now be in a position to offer a more informed assessment of the whole package. Bearing in mind the expectations you have just identified in Activity 29, how does what you currently deliver compare?

A clean slate

If the output customers want is very different from the output you currently deliver – or if it's a completely new output – you may need to wipe the slate clean and design the process from scratch, starting with the customer and working back through the organization. Re-engineering imagines that you have no technological, financial, human, or geographical constraints and just seeks the best way to deliver the output.

WHERE RE-ENGINEERING FITS IN

Macdonald (1995) sets out the spectrum of business process efforts as ranging from:

- **incremental improvement** (tweaking and improving existing processes to do the same thing better – as promoted by Kaizen and total quality approaches), through
- **process redesign** (focusing on major processes and the output for customers, this challenges and rationalizes existing processes, to optimize the available resources and technology), to
- **process re-engineering** (creating a completely new network of core processes and priorities) which involves:

The fundamental rethinking and radical design of business processes to achieve dramatic improvements in critical contemporary measures of performance such as cost, quality, service and speed.

(Hammer and Champy, 1993)

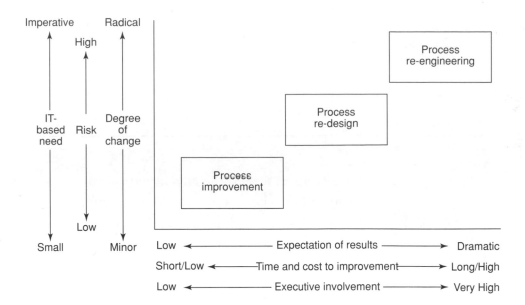

Figure 20

Essentially, the techniques and tools are the same as those for process improvement and the process looks similar on paper as shown in Figure 21.

Process re-engineering is likely to change radically the way the organization is structured, what it delivers, and how it delivers it, as well as the way people are managed. It is generally considered the choice of organizations whose continued existence might be in doubt if they did not reinvent themselves. Champy (1995) suggests that there are two main reasons for undertaking re-engineering: greed and fear (and the greatest of these is fear ...).

ACTIVITY 30

Where do you think your organization's process efforts would lie on the spectrum between incremental improvement and process re-engineering? Why?

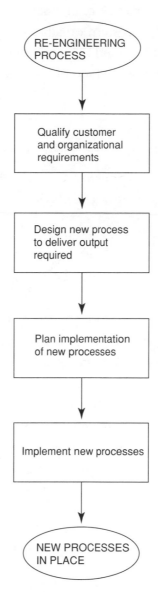

Figure 21 Re-engineering process

In practice, most organizations will combine process re-engineering with process improvement; quick wins will build momentum for the initiative; and once the processes have been re-engineered, continuous improvement will be essential to sustain results.

Re-engineering results

The risk of re-engineering may be higher; but the gains are higher too. The capability and product or service offered by international competitors – particularly from the Pacific Basin – have left Western organizations far behind in the global marketplace. We need some way to 'leapfrog' back into the lead.

Business process re-engineering offers just such a promise, and research shows that western organizations are taking it up. Sixty-nine per cent of US organizations and 75 per cent of European organizations are currently attempting some kind of re-engineering.

Leicester Royal Infirmary

Maull *et al.* (1995) cite the example of the arthritis clinic process at Leicester Royal Infirmary. Prior to re-engineering, the process would have looked something like Figure 22 (although the following is necessarily simplified).

All patients saw the consultant to start with, but 80 per cent of patients required urine, blood and X-ray tests, which were each conducted by someone different. So the patient trekked round the different departments, waiting for results in each, before returning to see the same consultant with their results, to hear their diagnosis and treatment. The re-engineering team designed the new process (Figure 23) so that the patient would be greeted and tested by a single cross-trained member of staff, before seeing the consultant, with all test results complete. So patients now spent an average of one hour in the hospital, compared with four hours before re-engineering.

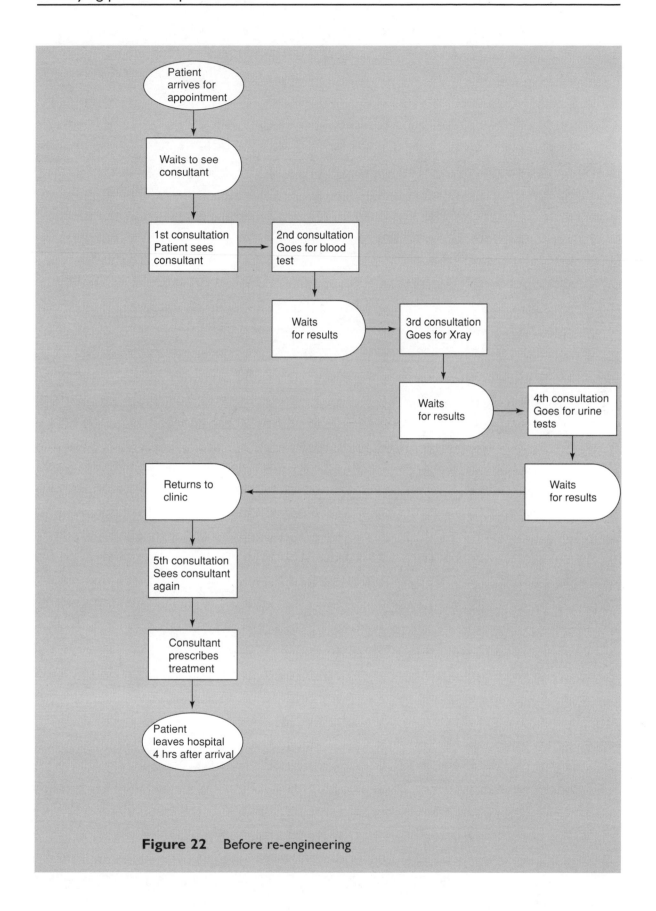

Figure 22   Before re-engineering

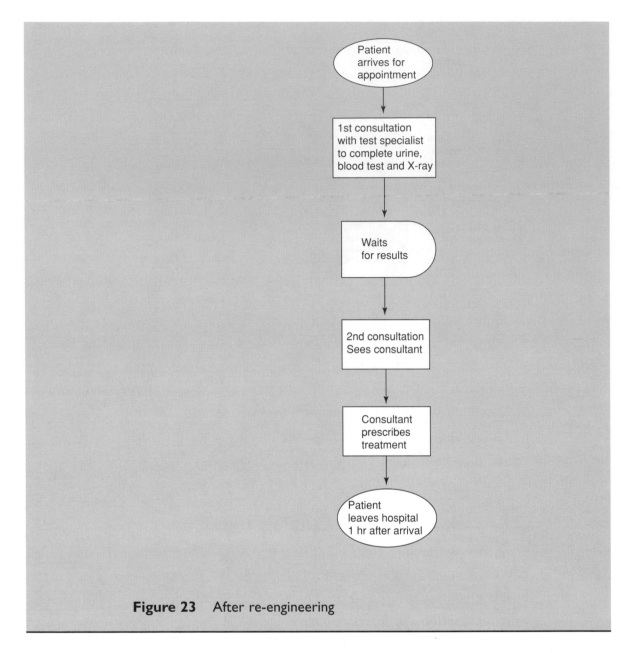

Figure 23   After re-engineering

Other oft-cited examples of success include the following case studies.

CASE STUDY

Pilkington Optronics

Following re-engineering, customer delivery performance rose from 20 per cent to 80 per cent; and a pre-re-engineering loss of £10 million in 1988/89 compares with a post-re-engineering profit of £5 million in 1993/94

(Harrison and D'Vaz, 1995).

Rank Xerox UK

Following re-engineering order time was reduced from thirty-three days to six days, and the company experienced a 20 per cent growth in revenue (although some of this may be due to changes in market factors)

(Davenport and Short, 1990).

Royal Bank of Scotland

Reputation for service was poor in 1991, but won 'a string of plaudits for service quality' in 1994, and profits rose from £6 million to £532 million in the same period

(Wellins and Rick, 1995).

Kodak

The company reduced the time to bring new products to market by 50 per cent and the costs of tooling and manufacture by 25 per cent

(Harrison and D'Vaz, 1995)

The focus of re-engineering efforts on either side of the Atlantic tends to be different. In the USA the main impetus is competitive pressure; in Europe, the emphasis is on cost-cutting (Champy, 1995).

ACTIVITY 31

What are the factors influencing your organization to improve or re-engineer its processes?

The downside

Re-engineering does have risks, however:

- the new processes may be liable to all sorts of '**teething trouble**' which because of the scope of the change, may have significant impact on customers, suppliers and employees
- re-engineering requires considerable investment and organizational effort; it takes a long time to design, implement and then to train people for the new processes (around two years for a major change). The **returns may not justify the investment**
- the new processes may **clash with the engrained culture, values or strategy**, resulting in confusion and obstruction of the change effort (congruence or alignment is absolutely essential for successful change)
- the disruption may be counterproductive if it **undermines employee morale**, and confidence in the organization and in management (see Section 6)
- it is fair to assume that the more radical the change, the greater the **resistance** to it (see Section 6)
- there is a **conflict of interests** if people are being asked to work out more efficient and effective ways to do things in order to reduce headcount – few will want to design themselves out of a job (more about this in Section 6)

There are claims that as many as 70 per cent of re-engineering efforts are unsuccessful (Hammer, 1990) – although this figure is liable to several interpretations. Is it that the initiative is poorly managed? Or was the organization failing anyway? The strategy itself is extreme; organizations that undertake it are likely to be under intense pressure and in difficult market conditions. James Champy has highlighted problems that may arise 'when work gets re-engineered and management doesn't' (about which, more in Section 6).

ACTIVITY 32

What concerns might you have about business process re-engineering and what approaches could you adopt to meet those concerns?

Guidelines for success

Carr and Johansson (1995) identified the following best practices for successful business process re-engineering (list abridged from Harrison and D'Vaz, 1995):

- an extremely compelling need to change
- executive level support
- readiness to change
- create buy in
- top-notch teams
- a structured framework for introduction
- use consultants effectively
- link goals to corporate strategy
- listen to the 'voice of the customer'
- select the right processes for re-engineering
- don't do too many (one to three macro processes at once)
- understand the 'as-is' of the processes
- choose and use the right metrics to measure performance
- understand the risks and develop contingency plans
- plan for continuous improvement once the process has been re-engineered

ACTIVITY 33

Use the above guidelines to audit your organization's process efforts. Where are you now? What would you need to do if you wanted to take re-engineering further in your organization?

Summary

Once you have documented and got to grips with the process **as it is now**, you can begin to work out where improvements are required, and what form these may take.

The process map may highlight opportunities for **streamlining** – eliminating duplication and redundant steps, smoothing and simplifying the flow, or changing the order to parallel process different tasks. **Error-proofing** is another technique to reduce variance and standardize outputs in the process. **Critical examination** offers a comprehensive and systematic approach, challenging every element of the process.

More innovative possibilities may be generated by focusing on ways **to shorten the cycle time**; or using the **fishbone diagram** to get to the bottom of problems and identify root causes (as opposed to presenting symptoms).

Such incremental improvements may be insufficient, however, where the current process is delivering the wrong outputs for customers or the organization. Redesign or **radical re-engineering** may be required, starting with a definition of customer requirements, and then working back through the organization to create the process that will deliver them.

Although the **rewards** are high, there are **risks** attached to re-engineering – the scope of the change; the human consequences; and the heavy investment required. However, business process re-engineering is now well established; there is a substantial body of case study research and best-practice guidelines to offer support to organizations intending to follow this route.

Section 5 Identifying system improvements

In this section of the workbook, we focus on the systems that support the process. We explore the opportunities that the process mapping exercise has revealed to check outputs during the process, what to measure, and who should measure it. We introduce and explain five analytical tools – ticksheets, bar charts, Pareto charts, line graphs, control charts – and how they can help. We consider what you will do with all these measures – putting them to effective use to control and improve the process. Finally, we review the opportunities presented by benchmarking to compare your processes and outputs with similar processes in your own organization or beyond.

When you have worked through this section of the workbook, you will be able to:

- identify quality checkpoints along the process
- select appropriate measures
- ensure appropriate review systems are in place
- benchmark the process against similar processes elsewhere in the organization or in external organizations

Where this section fits

Having documented the process as it now operates, the next step is to identify potential for improvement in the process, in the systems that support it, or in the people who operate it.

Analysing the current situation and generating ideas for improvements is likely to be quite a lengthy and complex business, covering all three areas of process capability – the process, the systems, and the people. However, for the sake of clarity, we have presented them sequentially in this workbook. Section 4 focused on the process itself; Section 6 will focus on the people. This section will focus on analysing and identifying improvements to the **systems** that support the process.

Why measure?

Measurements are key. If you cannot measure it, you cannot control it. If you cannot control it, you cannot manage it. If you cannot manage it, you cannot improve it.

(Harrington, 1991, p.82)

If processes exist to enable the organization to achieve its objectives and deliver outputs for customers, the better you do both these things, the greater your competitive advantage.

ACTIVITY 34

Identify some benefits of obtaining quality information about processes.

Knowing how you are doing – and where you are falling short – enables you to:

- understand the process better
- decide whether you need to change it
- decide how you need to change it
- evaluate the impact of changes
- sustain service and quality levels
- plan schedules for delivery

... so that you can improve the process and the way the output is delivered – and thereby increase your competitive advantage.

The advantage of measures is their objectivity: it's harder to argue with quantified evidence of below-par performance, or the need for process change. On the other hand, not everything can be measured in this strictly quantified way. If you focus attention only on things that can easily be measured you may end up measuring the wrong things.

'Insofar as hard figures are still unavailable,
our Mr Rendleman has written a poem that explores
the essence of the firm's situation.'
(by kind permission of *Training*, November 1994, p.15)

ACTIVITY 35

Identify some reasons why people might be reluctant to measure.

BARRIERS TO MEASUREMENT

In many instances, measurement simply doesn't happen. Why?

- because people don't realize **why** it's important
- because they don't know **what** to measure or **when**
- because they don't know **how**
- because they haven't got the **time**
- because they haven't got the **money** (and measurement alone adds no value to the output)

■ because they haven't got the **staff or other resources** (and unless someone takes responsibility, it won't happen)

■ because there's **nothing in it for them** if they do (and it may actually be penalizing them if they're not recognized and rewarded for doing the checks, and it stops them achieving their core tasks on which they are appraised)

ACTIVITY 36

What is the major obstacle to measurement of processes in your organization?

What do you measure?

In Section 3 we considered the factors that determine the success of the process – its effectiveness, efficiency and responsiveness. But how will you know whether your process is effective, efficient or responsive? What **evidence** or **indicators** will prove that it is?

Specific indicators can be identified that accurately correlate with efficiency or effectiveness (or lack of them) in the process or its outputs. Appropriate **metrics** (units of measurement) can then be decided for the indicators and the **standards** required, or the **range** of acceptable results. Then it's a question of measuring the indicators to evaluate actual process performance.

Management is responsible for providing sound measurement systems and appropriate feedback to help all do their jobs better. Management signals what is important by measuring the results.

(Harrington, 1991, p.169)

And – over time – the evidence suggests that you're likely to get what you measure.

Effectiveness indicators might include the following (with possible metrics in brackets):

- size (expressed in millimetres or acreage)
- quantity (expressed in crates)
- accuracy (number of errors or percentage within tolerances)
- customer satisfaction (expressed as a rating), or
- for the organization, employee retention (expressed as a percentage of staff)
- again for the organization, congruence with organizational values, strategy or specific objectives (expressed as a rating)

Efficiency indicators might include:

- profitability (expressed as £ per head; or percentage profit per order, or sales per floor area)
- output volume (litres per hour)
- utilization (percentage of time the equipment was in use)
- cycle time (days)
- waiting time (hours)
- waste or rejects (expressed as a percentage of total production)

Responsiveness indicators might include:

- frequency of scans (number per year)
- technologies in use (simple audit)
- special orders (as a percentage of standard orders)
- product to market time

EASE OF MEASUREMENT

Bear in mind the ease of collecting data, when you select the indicators in your process. Unless you make it easy to collect the data, it may not happen; or if it does, you will simply be adding cost, resources and time to your process. By themselves, data add no value; so limit your checks to only those data that are essential to control and manage the process. 'Nice to know' is simply costing you more with no prospect of returns.

ACTIVITY 37

What indicators do you use to track the effectiveness, efficiency and responsiveness of the process you documented in Section 3, Activity 24?

What metrics do you apply?

Have you specified the standards or range of acceptable results for each?

Having documented your process, can you identify other indicators and metrics that may be appropriate?

When do you measure?

Process improvements of any kind require considerable investment of time and effort; you'll want to know what difference they make. Quantify what the process delivered **before** improvement and what the process delivers **after** improvement, and compare the two. If all other things are equal, then any change may be attributed to the improvement you have made.

The process is continually delivering outputs to your internal and external customers. You need to know on an **ongoing basis** that what you deliver meets or exceeds their requirements. If there are problems, you need to know the extent of them, how frequently they arose, and how they impacted on the customer, so that you can take action. Measurement is still the answer.

AT THE END

The detailed output specification you develop with your customer will be one yardstick for the **eventual output** at the end of your process. But checking results at the end provides little information about the individual activities within the process. What it does tell you may be too late. By then, you could have wasted considerable energy and resources on an unacceptable output – a typical effect of 'inspected in' quality.

If you're considering the refunds process of your organization, for example, measuring results at the end may tell you that the refund took one full month longer than promised, but it doesn't tell you why – whether the branch office used the wrong form and had to resubmit, or head office delayed the cheque request, or it got lost in the mail. It doesn't tell you how efficiently each of the individual activities was completed, or whether the right output was delivered at every stage.

DURING THE PROCESS

If you want to build in quality, you need 'windows' on the process to track the ouput as it moves through the process. Then you can identify where any problems creep in, and take action as soon as possible to correct them, so that you don't waste time and resources on outputs that are not up to scratch. Your process map from Section 3 – and any improvements or redesign since – may have revealed opportunities for these kinds of checks within individual activities, or on handovers between different individuals, teams or departments. Which are the activities that have greatest impact on effectiveness, efficiency or responsiveness? These are likely to offer the most productive opportunities for monitoring.

ACTIVITY 38   F4

Take another look at the process map you drew in Section 3, Activity 24 and your answers to Activity 37.

How frequently do you measure your process against the indicators you have identified? (Once-off, every year, every month, every day?)

Indicator   **Frequency of measurement**

What opportunities can you see on your process chart for in-process monitoring?

Who measures?

Who does the measuring may seem obvious once you determine when and where you're going to measure the process. It makes sense to measure results as soon as possible after each critical activity; surely the best person to measure the results is whoever completes the task?

CONTROL ISSUES

Measurement is a method of control; as such it is 'politically loaded'. Control has traditionally been the preserve of the manager: managers control and organize; workers do. This may have had some bearing on reality in the ideal Taylorian factory, where myriad unskilled operators completed strictly limited mechanical tasks (but were never required to think about them) while managers told operators what to do (but were never required to do it themselves).

Today, people are better educated; social mores have changed and people may have higher expectations about the way they should be treated. The nature of work may also have changed; more workers are now employed in service or knowledge-based roles than in manufacturing. Managers may be thinner on the ground; and new organizational structures and increased participation may push responsibility down the line, to take up the slack. The output of knowledge workers in particular (professionals, consultants, advisers, analysts, etc.) is notoriously difficult to measure. So people in all areas of work may (theoretically) have greater scope for discretion and decision making.

SELF-FULFILLING PROPHESIES

However, the trend is patchy even within the same organization; and what happens in practice may differ substantially from the espoused policy. McGregor's research with Theory X and Theory Y (representing these two extremes of control or trust) has indicated that they may be self-fulfilling prophesies. If you believe your people are lazy, coerce them into work and keep checking up on them, they will grow to meet these expectations. On the other hand, if you believe your people are trustworthy and treat them so, they will generally become so (McGregor, 1960).

But when your job depends on your people achieving certain standards, how far are you prepared to trust them to vet outputs for themselves? Clarifying the indicators, how they are to be measured, and the acceptable range, should lessen the risk. There is, however, a cautionary tale.

CASE STUDY

A quality consultant was working with a parts manufacturer, and was shown round with some pride. 'This is Anna, our star operative. As you can see from this chart, 100 per cent of her sampled parts are within tolerances.' Impressed by this, the consultant asked to see her testing five random parts. Not one of the parts fell within acceptable tolerances. 'Oh,' she said, 'You'd be surprised how many I have to test sometimes, just to get five for the chart.'

So people need to understand the **purpose** of their self-checks, as well as what to do, when, and how.

ACTIVITY 39

Who could measure the relevant indicators you identified above? Who has the opportunity? What would they need to support their assessment and ensure accuracy and fairness. List the pros and cons of each option – in terms of the time required, the cost of that person's time, the likelihood of distortion, etc.

Indicator   Who measures   Support tools   Points for   Points against

Ticksheet (or checksheet)

Once you've decided what indicators to use, when you'll check them, and who will check them, you need to start thinking about **how** you'll collect the data, and how you'll present them, in order to facilitate any decisions you need to make.

Perhaps the simplest type of data collection (and often the quickest to use) involves a form designed so that all you have to do is tick in the box: every tick indicates one example of the relevant attribute.

Down the left-hand side, list outputs you are measuring – the parts manufactured, or the reports typed, or the individual projects. Across the top of the page are the categories of performance – the timescales, the measurement ranges, pass or fail, etc. For example, Figure 24 shows a ticksheet from a furniture workshop.

From the ticksheet, you can see that the workshop dealt with more coffee table orders than any other item; and not one took more than two days from receipt of order through to delivery of the finished goods. On the other hand, the rectangular table has a much more varied cycle time: you might want to investigate this and find out what's going on.

Cycle time Item	Less than 2 days	2–3 days	3–4 days	More
Circular table	✓✓✓✓✓	✓✓		
Rectangular table	✓✓	✓✓✓	✓✓	✓
Coffee table	✓✓✓✓✓ ✓✓✓✓✓			

Figure 24   Furniture order turnaround (ticks)

Once you've gathered the basic data, especially if there are a lot of ticks in each category, you could add up the ticks and write in the actual numbers as shown in Figure 25.

Cycle time Item	Less than 2 days	2–3 days	3–4 days	More
Circular table	24	5		
Rectangular table	10	16	3	3
Coffee table	40			

Figure 25   Furniture order turnaround (numbers)

Another variant involves recording the actual measures in the columns (so that each row on the chart only contains the measures for a single item or output), but this is more prone to errors than a simple tick. Obviously, the design of the form will depend on what you are measuring. Before printing the ticksheets, however, do check out your design with the people who will use it, to make sure you get the information you want, and that it's easy to use.

ACTIVITY 40

EITHER: Find an example of a ticksheet currently in use in your organization, and talk to the individuals who use it. Is it collecting the right information? How easy is it to complete? How could it be improved?

OR: Design a new ticksheet to measure one of your key indicators identified from earlier activities in this section. Ask the people who will use it to test it out, and use any feedback to amend your ticksheet accordingly.

Graphs

Once you've got all your raw data gathered, you'll need to start working out what it means. Columns of figures or ticks are difficult to read and difficult to compare. Graphs, on the other hand, have the advantage of facilitating comparisons and revealing trends.

BAR CHART (OR HISTOGRAM)

Use this when you are **comparing frequency, percentage or volume** in different categories. Label the X (horizontal axis) with the categories you are measuring. Label the Y (vertical axis) with the volume, percentage or frequency measures. Add up the volume frequency of each category from your ticksheet. Then draw in blocks representing that volume or frequency. Colour coding the blocks enables you to differentiate between groups in each category. For example, the bar chart in Figure 26 plots total sales by three different teams over four quarters. You can compare performance for a single team across all quarters; and compare the performance of all teams in each quarter.

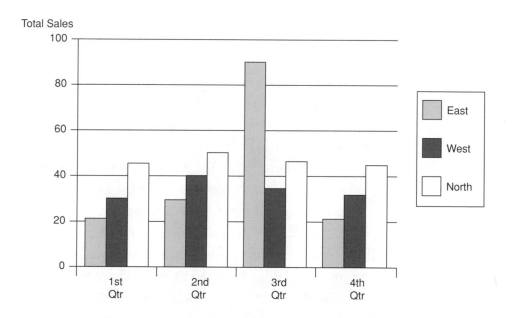

Figure 26   Example of a bar chart

EITHER: Find an example of a bar chart currently in use in your organization. Who prepares this? Talk to them about how it is used, and where and how they obtain the raw data. How could it be improved?

OR: Prepare a bar chart to illustrate some key information about your process. Who needs this information? Test out your bar chart with them.

PARETO CHART

The Pareto chart capitalizes on a general rule of thumb – Pareto's 80/20 rule. This suggests that 80 per cent of the problems (or whatever you're measuring) are attributable to 20 per cent of the possible causes (or whatever category you're using). So, for example, 80 per cent of the sales might come from 20 per cent of your customers; you spend 80 per cent of your time on 20 per cent of the projects; 80 per cent of the returns are caused by 20 per cent of the faults. If you know **which** 20 per cent are causing 80 per cent of the problems, you can focus your attention accordingly.

A Pareto chart is a bar chart in which the Y (vertical) axis represents percentage. Convert your results into percentages and draw bars representing each category on the graph. Arrange the bars in order of height, from the tallest on the left, nearest the Y (vertical) axis to the shortest on the right, furthest away from the Y axis.

Then, starting with the first bar, plot a **cumulative total** above each bar. Add the total for the first bar to the total for the second bar, and plot this cumulative total as a point immediately above the second bar. Then add this total to the total for the third bar, and plot a point immediately above that, and so on. Then join up the points. You should end up with bars along the bottom, and a line across the top of the chart, something like Figure 27.

Figure 27 represents the faults discovered in a product: you can see that 84 per cent of the problems stem from a faulty fuse or faulty wiring. If you're short of time, or have to decide which to tackle first, focusing on just these two will cure 84 per cent of the problem.

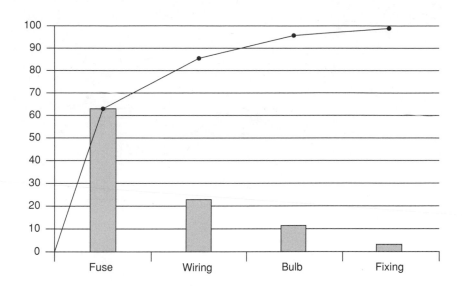

Figure 27   Example of a Pareto chart

ACTIVITY 42

Use the data from the bar chart used in Activity 41. Convert them into percentages, and draw a Pareto chart. What does this tell you about the process?

LINE GRAPH

Use a line graph when you need to **track trends over time**. Mark the X (horizontal) axis with the time frames, and the Y (vertical) axis with the volume, frequency, or percentage you are measuring. Then plot each measure on the chart, according to when it was taken, and join the points. Figure 28 illustrates an example of a line graph.

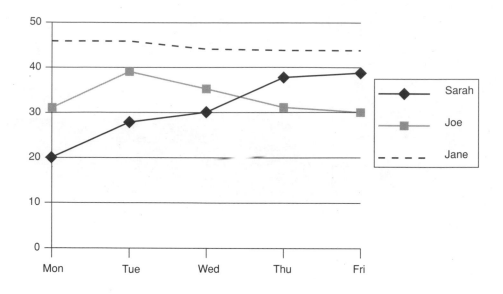

Figure 28   Example of a line graph

From Figure 28 you can see that while Sarah's figures are gradually rising over the week, the trend for the other two is in the opposite direction.

ACTIVITY 43

EITHER: Find an example of a line graph currently in use in your organization. Who prepares this? Talk to them about how it is used, and where and how they obtain the raw data. How could it be improved?

OR: Prepare a line graph to illustrate some key information about your process. Who needs this information? Test out your line graph with them.

CONTROL CHART

The control chart or statistical control chart is a tool frequently used in total quality. Like a line graph, it shows trends over time, but it also shows upper and lower limits of tolerance. It sounds complicated, but it's intended to make life easier, because it **highlights exceptions**, so that you know when action is required.

Start off by drawing a line graph. Add horizontal lines across the chart to represent the upper and lower limits of acceptable measurements, or tolerances. Plot your measures on the chart and join the points exactly as for a line graph. Any points outside the upper or lower limits are highlighted, as are any patterns (such as a repeated zig-zag, or a row of three rising or falling measures). Then you can take action accordingly.

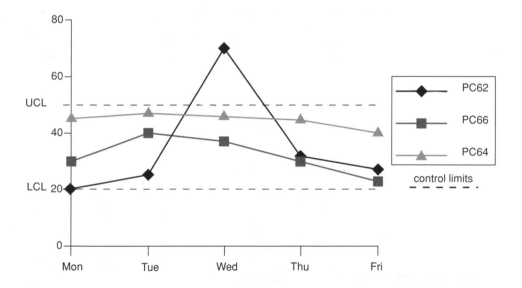

Figure 29   Example of a control chart

The control chart in Figure 29 plots the number of parts rejected as below standard. You can see that on Wednesday there were an exceptional number of PC62 rejects – approximately twenty-one more than the acceptable upper limit. You might want to investigate this: why is it happening, and why did it only affect PC62?

EITHER: Find an example of a control chart currently in use in your organization. Who prepares this? Talk to them about how it is used, and where and how they obtain the raw data. How could it be improved?

OR: Prepare a control chart to illustrate some key information about your process. Who needs this information? Test out your control chart with them.

Using the information

*By themselves, all the data in the world, even when analysed in the most sophisticated ways, accomplish nothing. In fact, data collection, data analysis and data storage, are activities that add no value **until the data are used to control, inform or improve a process**.*

(Harrington, 1991, p.194)

The whole point of measuring, and gathering data, is to monitor process performance so that you can identify **where** action is required and **what** action may be most appropriate.

Standards and targets

Once you know what results you actually get, you can decide what results you want. You can set **standards** and **targets**.

STANDARDS

Standards are the **minimum** acceptable levels of performance to satisfy your customer or the organization. In effectiveness measures, these are likely to be the standards your customer specified for the outputs. In efficiency measures, you may find that you need to set your own standards, based on your records of past performance, and the levels of profit or throughput required to break even on the process. Alternatively, benchmarking may help you to specify appropriate standards.

Harrington (1991) points out that half your work force will be 'below average'. The process therefore needs to be designed so that below average workers can deliver the outputs to minimum standards. If they can't, you may need to change your process so they can.

TARGETS

Targets are the **improvement goals** you set for the process. They are objectives designed to stretch, but also to reward – there's a sense of real achievement in hitting targets. This is the game you play when you decide you want to reduce your golf handicap to single figures, or get your weight down to 60kg. Targets may involve delivering more (or better) with the same resources; or using fewer resources to deliver the same (or better).

If you don't have targets, the only goal you will have is to be perfect. If your only objective is never to make another error, each time you do make an error, you have failed, and that soon becomes unmotivating.

(Harrington, 1991, p.182)

ACTIVITY 45

What standards are currently set for your process? Who sets them?

What targets are currently set for the same indicators? Who sets them?

What happens when you achieve them?

The feedback system

Taking the measures and preparing the charts is not just a one-off event. You'll need to know on an ongoing basis how your process is performing. So, having identified the key indicators, and the best method of collecting and presenting the data for interpretation, the next step is to **formalize** the data collection and graphing.

Set up a system that collects this data on a regular basis, and graphs it in the most appropriate manner, so that you can compare results with standards and targets. The system should specify exactly what should be checked, how frequently, and by whom – and what kinds of results should trigger action.

Once a system is in place, and responsibility is assigned for it, you won't have to start from scratch every time you want to collect this information. The right information should automatically be collected and presented in the right way at the right time, to provide the feedback you need to decide what to do and when to do it. And the staff, time and resources for the data collection and feedback system can be anticipated and factored into your plans, schedules and budgets.

ACTIVITY 46   F4

Use the form below to systematize your data collection and interpretation for your processes.

Details	Process 1	Process 2	Process 3	Process 4
Data to collect?				
How often?				
Who to collect?				
Report to whom?				
How to present?				
Who to generate?				
Standards set?				
Targets set?				
What triggers for action?				

Benchmarking

How do you know what targets to set? You may be able to specify targets based on 'best performance' currently achieved within the process. But – however stretching these targets are for the process itself – if they are lower than your competitors' targets, they're unlikely to bring competitive advantage.

Benchmarking involves comparing your process with best practice in similar processes elsewhere in the organization, in competitor organizations, in parallel but non-competing organizations, and/or in different industries using similar processes (see Figure 30).

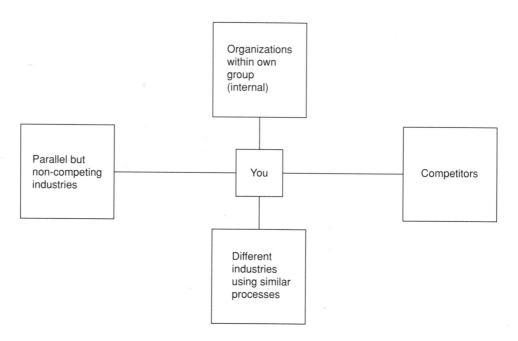

Figure 30   Who to benchmark

Because benchmarking shows what can be done, and gives everyone a chance to share ideas about their own work, it can be enormously motivating for the people involved. Where you cannot transplant the ideas directly, you may be able to modify or adapt them. Benchmarking can stimulate thinking about the process in new ways, and lead to more creative ideas for improvement. And it can lead to wider recognition for excellence within the process; even underperforming processes may have some excellent aspects.

CASE STUDY

Xerox benchmarked itself against its Japanese affiliate, Fuji-Xerox, and discovered that Fuji-Xerox was selling copiers cheaper than Xerox could manufacture them.

When **Ford** benchmarked its accounts payable function against Mazda, it found that while this required 500 dedicated staff at Ford, Mazda performed the task with just *five* people. Looking at Mazda's process enabled Ford to change the process and thereby cut staff numbers in this area by 75 per cent.

HOW TO DO IT

Figure 31 illustrates the benchmarking process.

The first task is to decide what you want to benchmark: select processes where you believe there is potential for improvement, or which consume most effort and resources. Document these processes and list the essential indicators – and current performance levels. You need to know your own processes thoroughly before you start to consider how others work. Identify benchmark comparators: this may be the most time consuming part of the process. Good places to start include benchmarking research bodies, trade associations and institutions, and suppliers and customers. Share your data with these comparators, and determine where differences arise, and why. (Do be careful when comparing figures – make sure you're comparing like with like.) Then, as with any measurement exercise, use the information to make a decision and take appropriate action.

Table 1 shows the Institute of Management's suggestions for successful benchmarking.

Table 1 Institute of Management checklist: a programme for benchmarking

Do	Don't
■ ensure senior management support	■ underestimate the need for willingness to change
■ ensure it is a team activity	■ be too ambitious at the start
■ understand your own processes first	■ view benchmarking as a tool for short-term gains

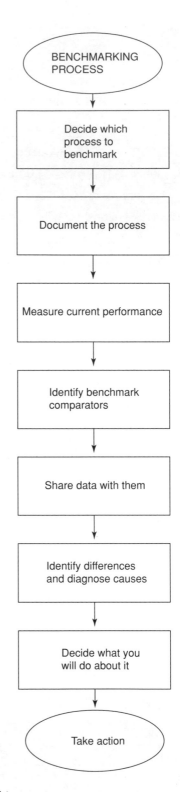

Figure 31   Benchmarking process

TAKE YOUR TIME

This tour of benchmarking is necessarily brief. If you are seriously considering benchmarking (and it can be a powerful tool for key processes), we recommend that you invest some time finding out more about the techniques:

- talk to organizations that are already benchmarking their processes
- read books or articles on the subject – such as *Practical Benchmarking*, by Sarah Cook, published by Kogan Page (1995); or 'How to build a benchmarking team' by M.J. Spendolini, *Journal of Business Strategy*, vol.14, no.2, Mar/Apr, 1993, pp. 53–57.
- contact the Benchmarking Council or the Benchmarking Centre

ACTIVITY 47

Which processes might benefit from benchmarking in your organization?

Which organizations might offer useful benchmarking comparators?

What might you be able to offer them?

One last word on the subject: benchmarking is a two-way deal. It's no good imagining you'll sweep in, pick your competitor's brains and steal their good ideas, and get clean away. They'll be looking for your ideas too: consider what you can offer them.

Summary

If processes exist to enable the organization to achieve its objectives and deliver outputs to customers, the better you do this, the greater your competitive advantage. But you need **indicators** and **measures** to compare process performance; otherwise how will you know you're improving?

For many organizations, the difficulty arises in **selecting** the indicators, or in **measuring** them. Select indicators that accurately correlate with the quality you want to measure – whether this is effectiveness, efficiency, or responsiveness. However, measurement alone will add no value to your process: so focus on essential measures only.

It's no good measuring the output only at the end of the process; by then, you may have wasted considerable time and resources on an output that is not acceptable. For optimum control, there must be windows on the process that enable you to check outputs as the process flows through the organization.

Measurement is best done as soon as possible after the activity; the best person to carry out the checks may be the person who completes the activity. However, this requires a degree of trust which may be lacking in the organization or in individual managers. There may be concerns about accuracy of test results which may make peer evaluation, or other arrangements, more appropriate.

Tools that may be helpful to quantify and display process data include:

- ticksheet
- bar chart
- Pareto chart
- line graph
- control chart

The purpose of gathering this data is to inform decision making and lead to more productive action.

Standards are the minimum acceptable levels of performance in each indicator to satisfy the customer or the organization. **Targets** are improvement goals you set for the process. Both should help control and improve process results.

Data collection and analysis is not a one-off; the process must be monitored and reviewed on an ongoing basis. The **feedback system** must be formalized so that the right information is automatically gathered and analysed at the right time to facilitate action planning.

Benchmarking can help keep the organization in touch with best practice in the organization, in the process type, or in the industry, resulting in more challenging stretch targets and the sharing of innovative ideas. However, this can never be a 'quick fix'. Relationships of trust with competitors or other outside organizations take time to develop; and benchmarking partners will expect to learn something from you in return.

Section 6   Identifying people improvements

In this section of the workbook, we consider what people contribute to the process and why managers may fail to actualize this potential. We review the factors that enable people to deliver process results: information, resources, incentives, skills training, intrinsic capacity, and motivation. Manipulating these factors may therefore help to enhance process performance. In the second half of the section, we explore the issues that the process approach may raise: conflicts of individual and organizational interests; changing roles and responsibilities (including the future of management); and the challenge to (or congruence with) corporate culture.

When you have worked through this section of the workbook, you will be able to:

- consider what people contribute to the process
- recognize what people need from management and the organization in order to actualize the potential of the process
- recall attitudes to change and tactics to facilitate acceptance
- consider the implications of the process approach for teams, for management and for the organization itself

Where this section fits

Having documented the process as it now operates, the next step is to identify potential for improvement in the process, in the systems that support it, or in the people who operate it.

Analysing the current situation and generating ideas for improvements is likely to be quite a lengthy and complex business, covering all three areas of process capability – the process, the systems and the people. However, for the sake of clarity, we have presented them sequentially in this workbook. Section 4 focused on the process itself; Section 5 on systems; and here in Section 6, we consider the people aspects of processes, and how you as a manager can help people to deliver improved process performance.

People matter

If process innovation is to succeed, the human side of change cannot be left to manage itself. Organisational and human resource issues are more central than technology issues to the behavioural changes that must occur within a process.

(Davenport, 1993, p.96)

As we've said before, processes cannot achieve anything on their own; people operate the processes. Your process can be replicated by your competitors. What distinguishes your process from your competitors' process is the people who operate it – their unique combination of knowledge, skills and attitudes and the collective culture of the organization as a whole. However, there may be a tendency in process management to focus on the practical, technical elements of the process; and to pay too little attention to the human side.

ACTIVITY 48

Why do you think people issues are often ignored? What steps can be taken to improve this?

WHY?

This inattention to people may stem from the tradition of Taylorian management early this century, when operatives in predominantly mass production processes were manipulated almost as interchangeable factors of production. Tasks were broken down into the smallest possible chunks that required the least possible element of skill or personal judgement, in an effort to standardize production. The contribution of the individual to this mix was minimal, and consequently might be ignored with impunity.

This is no longer the case. More people are involved in service and knowledge-based industries where the contribution of the individual is the output for customers. In production environments, increasing automation and computerization mean that the remaining human tasks may be less routinized, and more concerned with identifying and handling exceptions. New organizational structures and increasing participation may push responsibility down the line. It is no longer enough simply to complete a given task; the individual is the prime value adder and output creator. The contribution of the individual is therefore central to the performance of any process.

Re-engineering has made businesses increasingly reliant on the skills, imaginations, commitment, values and behaviour of their employees. It has also transformed their employees' work, giving them more authority and the work more content, interest and complexity.

(Champy, 1995, p.154)

EMOTIONAL TIMEBOMB?

Part of the hesitation in dealing with the human aspects of processes may stem from discomfort in the face of human emotions, and a sense that people are more difficult to deal with and much less predictable than tasks or things.

We have already mentioned this aspect in Section 3. Work may be a defining factor in our perceptions of our self and sense of self-worth. Work underwrites our life decisions and lifestyles – our homes, family and relationships, hobbies and holidays. We invest a lot of our time, energy, and creativity in it. It may be one way of giving meaning to life, if we feel that we are doing something worth while. Our behaviour at work may express our deepest values and beliefs. Work may validate the individual within a wider context; it may secure recognition and reward; it may also enhance status. So challenging or changing what people do (which is a fundamental precept of process management) may seem to challenge or threaten a whole way of life.

So people may feel a terrible sense of loss when faced with change in their work tasks. Elisabeth Kubler-Ross (1989), a writer and counsellor with considerable experience of dealing with loss and grief, suggests people move through phases:

- **denial** (This has nothing to do with me. We're doing all right; we don't need to change)
- **anger** (I've had it up to here with these new fads. This is asking too much. I've slogged my guts out and now you want more)
- **bargaining** (Well OK, so long as .... Let's work out a compromise)
- **fear** (What if I'm not up to it? I don't know if I can cope)

- **resignation** (I guess if it's going to happen anyway, I'll have to go along with it)

Depending on their experiences, and the impact of the change, people may also experience:

- **hope** (So things will be better in future)
- **enthusiasm** (This is the best thing that's happened. Look what we can do now)

The phases aren't necessarily sequential; people may zig-zag between them, or start enthusiastic, and loop back through fear and anger when they realize just what's involved. They may feel some phases more than others, or even leap straight in at hope and enthusiasm. And everyone may be different.

'ACTING OUT' THE EMOTIONS

These emotions have a strong influence on how people actually behave at work: enthusiasm may lead to a missionary fervour; fear, anger, and sheer bewilderment may lead to almost subversive resistance.

CASE STUDY

Fowler and Graves (1995, p.49) cite one example of this. A defence supply company was earning a substantial proportion of its revenue from repair of its own equipment. Improving the quality of that equipment would therefore – in the eyes of the contracts manager – eliminate the guaranteed revenue this generated. So the contracts manager did everything in his power to resist the change – and nearly got himself sacked in the process.

ACTIVITY 49

Think back to a major organizational change you have experienced in the past. How did you feel about it, and how did you feel you were treated?

How will you use this experience to help you deal more effectively with the people involved in the process you manage?

Bringing people on board

You and other members of the process improvement team may spend a great deal of time thinking about the process, how it works and how to do it better. But not everyone has been with you at every step of the way. So you need to build ownership.

Share your thinking about how the process currently operates, the need for change and what you're trying to achieve. You may have lived with the reasons and the possibilities for the last three months; it'll take more than a single meeting or memo detailing the changes to bring people on board. Communication must be an ongoing process in itself. Give people time.

Top management typically over-estimates the degree of co-operation it will get and under-estimates the transition costs. Among the by-products of significant restructuring are discontinuity, disorder and distraction – all of which tend to reduce productivity.

(Rosabeth Moss Kanter, 1990, p.345)

Where change is involved, shock or emotional reactions may prevent people from hearing what you say: they'll interpret it according to their own concerns. You say 'efficiency', and they hear redundancies. You say 'improve the process' and they hear a criticism of how they're doing it now. So think about where they are now, and tailor your message accordingly. Tell them what's in it for them. Acknowledge and address their underlying concerns. Repeat the message. Use different media, different words, different perspectives.

FEEDBACK

Feedback can be a powerful tool as the changes are implemented, communicating the results of the process, and keeping up the momentum of the initiative. But it needs to be meaningful for the person who receives it.

CASE STUDY

At an IBM site in Havant, providing each assembly operator with final test feedback on the units each had produced led to a major decrease in defects. They could identify with their own work, and took pride in beating their previous results.

At a retail store in the Midlands, talking about theft and loss had failed to get people excited about the steady drain of profits. At the next team meeting, the manager drove a top-of-the-range BMW onto the shop floor. 'That's how much theft and loss cost us last month.' The team still think of theft and loss in these terms: they're aiming to get it down to a Mini – or even a mountain bike.

ACTIVITY 50

Who do you need to bring on board? Why do you think they might not follow procedures?

Supporting people

Managing processes must include dealing with everything people bring to the process – with their creativity and their feelings – as well as the logical and technological elements of the process. Only then can you begin to actualize the potential performance of the process.

Most people come to work wanting to do a good job. Harrington (1991) suggests that people deviate from a prescribed process because:

1 they **misunderstand** the procedures
2 they **don't know** the procedures
3 they don't understand **why** they should follow them
4 they find a **better** way of doing things
5 the procedure as documented is **too hard** to do
6 they don't have the **knowledge or skills**
7 they were **trained** to do it differently
8 someone **told** them to do it differently
9 they don't have the **tools**
10 they don't have the **time**

GILBERT'S MODEL

There are no guaranteed tools to get this right; each manager must select and use the tactics that seem appropriate for the workers and the situation. However, one model proposed by the American T. F. Gilbert (1978) and illustrated in Figure 32, may help to quantify the factors you need to consider, and offer possibilities to help you optimize the contribution people can make in your process.

INFORMATION	RESOURCES	INCENTIVES
Do they know:	Do they have:	Do they receive:
■ what is involved?	■ the right structure or organization to achieve objectives?	■ appropriate rewards and recognition for doing things right?
■ what they are aiming for?	■ the supplies, tools, equipment, time and staff to do it?	■ no **penalities** for doing it right?
■ what is expected of them?	■ systems and standard procedures to help them do it?	■ no rewards for doing it wrong?
■ how their bits fit in?	■ access to support if they get stuck?	
■ how they're doing?		
■ it's the truth and do they believe it?		
KNOWLEDEGE AND SKILLS	**CAPACITY**	**MOTIVATION**
Do they have the knowledge and skills:	Do they have the:	Do they:
■ to know what to do?	■ self-confidence and emotional capacity?	■ have autonomy?
■ for process analysis and improvement?	■ intellectual capacity?	■ actually WANT to do the tasks?
■ to work effectively in a team?	■ physical capacity	■ CARE about the results?
■ to complete the technical and operational tasks in the process?		■ OWN the process?

Figure 32 Human performance model (adapted from Gilbert, T. F., *Human Competence*)

ACTIVITY 51

Work through the six boxes in Gilbert's model, and check what factors are currently supporting the people who operate your process.

Identify any gaps, and consider how these could be remedied to help people operate the process more effectively, efficiently and responsively.

Motivation and incentives

Of all the factors in Gilbert's model, there may be most ambiguity around motivation and incentives. Managers may think that if they offer more incentives, people will be more motivated. But the two are quite different.

Incentives are what the organization offers; you may be able to change these. You can remove frustrations, or work people don't like; and enhance the rewards such as recognition, privilege, or pay. Get your incentives right and you may be able to persuade people to comply with the process. But you won't automatically tap into people's intimate knowledge of their own inputs and how the process works in practice; and people won't necessarily care enough to operate the process thoughtfully, or contribute their own ideas. You can buy someone's time, but that doesn't win their hearts.

Motivation is the natural drive or affinity an individual has towards (or away from) particular work or interests. When people are motivated to achieve something, they transcend compliance to access creativity, commitment and caring about how the process performs. Which, of course, is exactly what you need when you want to improve it.

How can you affect motivation? A 'pep' talk won't do the trick if it's something inherent in the individual. Research suggests that the following dimensions may influence motivation:

- **skill variety** (the range of skills involved in the tasks)
- **task identity** (the completeness of a task. For example, you may find building a complete car more satisfying than fitting a single part on any number of cars for the same period of time)
- **task significance** (the difference it makes)
- **autonom**y (control over the way the work is carried out)
- **feedback**

So, if you want to enhance individual motivation, consider what scope there is to adjust one or more of these elements in the way that work is allocated.

ACTIVITY 52

Think back to a time when you were particularly demotivated at work (or at school or university). Which element in the above list was at fault, and how did you change the balance?

Conflict of interests?

So far, the assumption has been that if something is good for the process and the organization, it will ultimately be good for the individuals involved. This may not be the case.

The association of re-engineering with 'downsizing' and redundancies is not accidental; the majority of European efforts in this direction have been geared to cutting costs, and labour remains a major factor of costs. Although reducing staff may not be the prime objective of re-engineering, it may be a natural consequence of doing things more efficiently – achieving more with less.

IS MY JOB AT RISK?

Harrington (1991) highlights the dilemma:

Management cannot expect people to evaluate the business processes fairly and look for ways to improve them if it means that they or the person working beside them will be laid off. We believe that management should develop a no-layoff policy ... Without this type of assurance, management cannot expect the full co-operation of the members of the performance improvement team or their management ... people will hide waste to protect themselves, their friends, and their employees.

(Harrington, 1991, p.53)

While the logic of his premise is undisputable, the solution he suggests may seem more problematic.

PRODUCTION VERSUS CAPABILITY

Stephen Covey (1992) highlights the need for balance between **production** (actual outputs or productivity) and production **capability** (the asset that produces the golden egg). In organizational terms, people are your production capability; cutting staff too drastically may compromise your ability to increase production when things pick up, or even to sustain existing levels of production. The result is a kind of corporate anorexia from which the organization gradually sinks into terminal decline.

(According to research conducted by the American Management Association) only 47 per cent of companies reporting workforce reductions since 1990 realised any increase in operating profits within a year following the reductions. Long term, only 46 per cent reported increased profits. Only one-third ... reported an increase in worker productivity.

(David Stamps, 1996)

Where companies do show a gain in profit or productivity following a cut in staffing, they have generally expanded their training efforts at the same time – investing again in the production capability of the workforce.

What are the prospects of redundancy as a result of your process improvement effort? What realistic assurances can you therefore offer your staff to allay fears about job security?

Roles and responsibilities

The process approach typically pushes power down the line to analyse, diagnose, and change the way work is done. The aim is to build autonomy, ownership and acceptance of any change, as well as increasing the quality of any change. However:

Don't expect people to change how they behave unless you change what they do; that is, their work must be designed to allow them to act differently.

(Champy, 1995, p.110)

There are implications in this for everyone concerned.

EMPOWERING OR DUMPING?

Bear in mind that not everyone wants increased responsibility for processes. It's convenient to be told what to do – less taxing, less tiring – and there's always someone else to blame if anything goes wrong. Besides, they're not paid for the responsibility ... There is a fine line between empowerment and being 'dumped on' and the main difference lies in how it's perceived by the individual.

ACTIVITY 54

Think back to a time when you were obliged to take responsibility for something you didn't want to do.

How did you feel about this?

And how did you deal with it?

What might have helped you come to terms with the responsibility?

You may have found that support and encouragement from your manager gave you confidence and the will to complete the task. Rewards or personal recognition may have gone some way to compensate for the effort required.

CASE STUDY

Champy (1995) cites AT&T, where every suggestion that directly improves performance is rewarded – up to a maximum of $10 000. The result is that two-thirds of the entire workforce submits at least one improvement per year (and 98 per cent of these suggestions are implemented).

TEAM POWER

In much of the literature on quality and process approaches, teamness is next to godliness – the greatest good. And it is true that empowered teams can produce extraordinary results, much greater than the sum of their individual parts. However:

Teams and workgroups have a shady side ...They can, for example, waste the time and energy of members rather than use them well. They can enforce norms of low rather than high productivity. They sometimes make notoriously bad decisions. Patterns of destructive conflict can arise, both within and between groups. And groups can exploit, stress and frustrate their members – sometimes all at the same time.
(J. Richard Hackman, 'The design of work teams', in Lorsch, J.W. (ed.), *Handbook of Organizational Behaviour*, 1987, cited in Davenport, 1993, p.102)

ACTIVITY 55

How strong is the team identity among your process team, and how does it manifest itself?

How might you reduce the risk of:

■ dissipation of time and energies

■ norms of low productivity and a rejection of 'rate-busting'?

■ groupthink?

■ destructive competition and conflict?

WHERE DOES THIS LEAVE THE MANAGER?

The internal power shift implicit in passing process responsibility down the line may leave the manager in a quandary, too. If teams are responsible for satisfying their customers' needs, deciding where action is required and agreeing that action, what is left for managers to do?

For us managers, nothing seems sure any more, neither our professional know-how nor our career paths – and certainly not our job security ... Management has joined the ranks of the dangerous professions.

(Champy, 1995, pp.6–7)

Champy goes on to articulate the new 'ordeal of management':

- nothing is simple any more ...
- whatever we do is not enough ...
- everything is in question ...
- everyone must change ...

Managers are not exempt from the emotional responses to loss we considered earlier.

When teams take responsibility for the process, managers have the opportunity to move into a more facilitating and coaching role. This involves a change of style and tasks they may find foreign or difficult. Managers may lose the direct contact with the customer and the work that brought them personal satisfaction and promotion in the first place. And what managers contribute – which consolidates their own sense of self-worth and achievement – becomes harder to quantify. The Chinese say that the sign of a good leader is that when his people accomplish their goal, they say 'We did it ourselves'. But it's hard to forgo recognition for your efforts.

Champy (1995) points out that management resistance alone may be enough to scupper the process changes:

The three vice presidents ... at a major computer company were thrilled that re-engineered work processes promised to cut product introduction time in half, raise customer retention rates by 20 per cent, and slice 30 per cent from administrative costs in their areas. They weren't thrilled enough, however, to willingly give up control of their fiefdoms and collaborate. Result: the re-engineering effort died a year after its inception.

(Champy, 1995, p.5)

So don't forget yourself when you work through Gilbert's model.

ACTIVITY 56

Run through Gilbert's model and identify what YOU need to enable you to fulfil the new role and responsibilities implicit in the process approach.

Cultural congruence

The process approach may present another dilemma for individuals and the organization as a whole. On the one hand, the aim is to challenge and change the way things are done, which may have a far-reaching impact on how people relate to each other and the way the organization operates. On the other hand, change is unlikely to take root where it is incompatible with established corporate culture – 'the way we do things round here'.

You may be familiar with the experience of coming back from a really stimulating and thought-provoking course, and wanting to put what you've learned into action, only to be squashed back into old moulds by the sheer force of cultural norms. This kind of chicken-and-egg situation may seem intractable, but there are precedents and possibilities.

ACTIVITY 57

List some key managment actions that you feel are important in the successful management of change.

For successful change:

- secure **top management commitment** to the changes – not just verbal support, but real modelling of what they mean for people day to day. If the process approach is so important, why aren't the top team using it to deliver their outputs – formulating strategy, values, vision?
- **involve the people** who will implement any changes, to build ownership
- create a compelling **vision** of how things will be – preferably a shared vision, in which people feel they have a stake
- emphasize where there is **continuity** – how the approach will align with the underlying values of the organization:

We have to provide something for people to hang onto, something that doesn't change.

(Champy, 1995, p.54)

- build '**pockets**' of the new way of doing things (self-sustaining teams). Evidence suggests that much change originates on the periphery of the organization, and only migrates to the centre when it is proven and accepted. You won't convert everyone overnight; but once you have a few teams delivering real results, this may stimulate interest and prepare the ground, building critical mass
- give people **time**. All the evidence suggest that a major cultural change may take anything from two to five years. Two years is probably the minimum for a major process re-design or re-engineering. And once the change is in place, no matter how beneficial, it will still take people time to build competence in the new way of doing things, and make the process work up to its full potential
- **celebrate successes**. Give people plenty of feedback so they know how they're doing and what's working

ACTIVITY 58

You initially considered the issue of cultural congruence in Section 2: how have your ideas changed since working through this section of the workbook?

Summary

When managing and improving processes, there may be a tendency to focus more on the technical aspects of processes rather than on people. This may stem from an outdated perception of people as factors of production. Today, more workers are operating in service or knowledge-based roles where their interaction with the customer is the output.

Part of the reason may be discomfort in the face of the emotional disturbance that may be occasioned by any change. Unless you bring people on board, resistance may prove destructive.

Gilbert's model is a reminder of the factors that managers may be able to influence in order to help people perform better:

- information
- resources
- incentives
- skills and knowledge (training)
- capacity
- motivation

Motivation is the key to accessing creativity and commitment; the degree of variety, identity, significance, autonomy and feedback inherent in the work may determine individual motivation.

The process approach may lead to a conflict of interests as people are expected to contribute to improvements that may ultimately make them redundant. Reducing staffing levels may also compromise production capability and contribute to a kind of corporate anorexia that jeopardizes the future existence of the organization.

Roles and responsibilities necessarily change with the introduction of a process approach. But not everyone will welcome the empowerment and responsibility entailed. **Team structure** alone is not sufficient to ensure productive teamworking; managers must be aware of the possible risks, and take action to minimize these. At the same time, managers must be prepared to relinquish their old roles and adopt a more facilitative stance.

The process approach may also pose a dilemma for the organization: on the one hand, it seeks to challenge the way things are done; on the other, change is unlikely to take root where it is incompatible with corporate culture.

Section 7   Next steps

So far in this workbook, we have diagnosed the need for business process improvement, documented the process, and identified possible improvements.

In this final section of the workbook, we explore the change-readiness of the organization and quantify the factors that may constrain or support any improvement option. We evaluate the risks and returns – including non-financial gains – of the possible improvements you have generated so far. We specify what the improvement must achieve (criteria of success) and use the weighted criteria worksheet to prioritize the improvements that seem most likely to deliver the results the organization requires. We then review techniques for planning the implementation and ongoing monitoring and review of the improvements you select.

When you have worked through this section of the workbook, you will be able to:

- identify the factors that may constrain or support the choices for improvement (force field analysis)
- evaluate the risks and returns of your improvement options (risk assessment and cost-benefit analysis)
- set selection criteria and prioritize the improvement options you wish to pursue (weighted criteria worksheet)
- plan implementation of selected improvements (action planning, Gantt chart)
- specify the indicators of success, and the programme of reviews to evaluate the effect of the improvements

What will help or hinder improvement?

So far, you may have generated a number of potential improvements. But you are not implementing these in a vacuum. The prevailing organizational context, its culture and values, its structure and technology, its resources and time horizons, may all serve to help or hinder the improvements you propose. It's important to acknowledge and try to quantify the factors that may help or hinder, so that you can make a fair assessment of what will be required to implement the improvement, and therefore whether it is worth while.

Budget is one of the most obvious constraints. You will want to make sure that what you invest is proportional to the returns you hope to achieve. In today's climate few organizations have 'spare' budget capacity; so funds may be even more limited. But financial constraints are not the only limitation.

For example, if the organization has just invested heavily in new plant, or a new office location, throwing it away and starting again from scratch may not be an option you can consider. Perhaps you need to demonstrate results quickly; time pressures may then become a factor in your assessment. On the other hand, if everyone acknowledges the need for change, you may find that the climate is particularly receptive to your improvement. And if it capitalizes on existing expertise, you may have an added advantage.

FORCE FIELD ANALYSIS

Force field analysis is a way of making these helping and hindering factors explicit, so that you can explore the weight they carry, and consider how to address them. As with brainstorming activities, this exercise is best done as a team to ensure that you capture different perspectives, and that everyone shares the same information.

On a flipchart, draw a large T shape with the crossbar at the top of the page and the upright extending to the bottom of the page. Write the improvement you're considering across the top of the T. Brainstorm all the factors supporting or helping implementation of this option and write these on the left-hand side. Brainstorm all the factors resisting or hindering the change, and write these on the right-hand side. Consider:

- organizational supports or hindrances (e.g. strategy, policies, procedures, structure, culture, values)
- people supports or hindrances (e.g. knowledge and skills, staffing levels, type of expertise, union involvement, colleagues, managers, or partners in the process)
- resources supports or hindrances (e.g. time horizons, budget, existing plant, tools or computer equipment)

When you have brainstormed all the supports and hindrances, try to rank them in terms of their impact; which will have greatest influence, and which least? Draw arrows underneath each towards the centre line, representing the weight of each support or hindrance. The factor which has most impact should have the longest arrow; and the least impact, the shortest.

Figure 33 shows the force field diagram of a furniture-maker based in Central London, whose improvement suggestion involves setting up a new making shop in Midbridge.

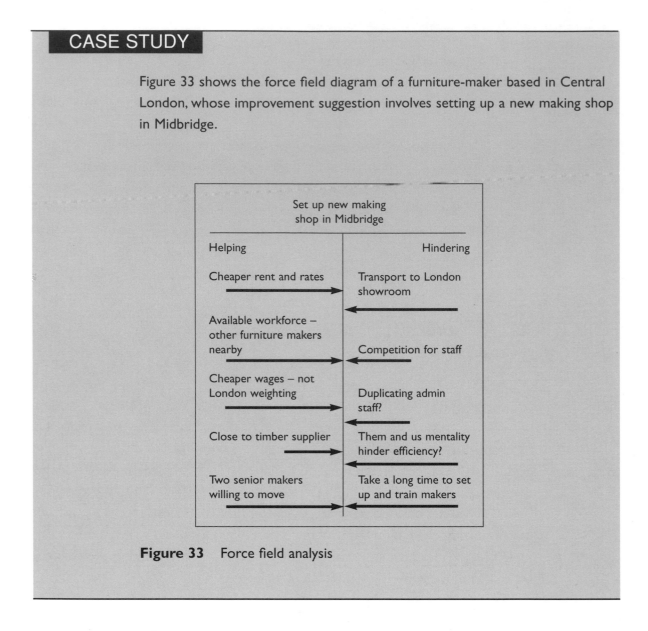

Figure 33   Force field analysis

At the moment, the forces are in balance, holding the vertical line in the centre of the page (where you are now). What might help you move the vertical line towards the right – towards actually setting up a new making shop in Midbridge, in our example? You could increase the helping forces, but that doesn't resolve the resistance issues. Even if you do steamroller them at the outset, they'll keep cropping up again as you implement the improvement. So think about how you could reduce or eliminate the hindrances.

ADDRESS THE ISSUES

While the brainstorming activity and ranking of supports or hindrances are necessary, it is this last, analysis stage that gives the tool its power. Don't skimp on the time it takes to work through each issue – keep asking 'why?' to identify the causes, then suggest what might address the root cause.

For example, in Figure 33, one cause of the 'them and us' mentality might be differences in terms and conditions. You might therefore suggest harmonizing terms and conditions of employment between Midbridge and London. Another cause might be the difficulty of communications; you might need to incorporate regular meetings. Continuing this exercise, transferring experienced senior makers to Midbridge might help to speed up training, and ensure continuity and parity, so that the culture and values remain consistent across both sites. And until Midbridge is fully operational, it may be necessary to retain the existing arrangements in some degree.

These are solutions you will need to include in the costings and any implementation plan.

ACTIVITY 59

Take one of your suggested improvements, generated through activities in the last three sections, and conduct a force field analysis to identify supporting and hindering factors.

Rank these factors, according to the impact they have.

Suggest how you might overcome the hindrances.

Assessing the risks

Some of the factors you identified in the force field analysis may already exist; others may be potential risks of any change.

Research by Maull *et al.* (1995) suggests that the greater the change, the greater the risk – and the greater the potential return:

Those organisations which took a radical view of the scope of change were taking much greater risks with their profitability and even survival. However, having gained substantial benefits in terms of lead time and cost reduction, they appear to have increased the likelihood of their long-term viability.

(Maull ct al., 1995, p.43)

Improvement efforts may always be something of a gamble: it is rarely possible to anticipate exactly how people will respond. There are so many interlocking elements holding the current process in place that changing one element may also have unforseen knock-on consequences elsewhere in the organization. But as far as possible, you need to anticipate these consequential impacts and quantify the risks, so that you can take these into account when weighing up the different options. Risk can be expressed as a formula:

Risk = impact $\times$ probability

Where the possible detrimental impact on the organization or customer is multiplied by the probability or likelihood of this occuring.

ACTIVITY 60

Take another look at your force field analysis, and identify any possible risks of this improvement option. Use the form below to record your answers.

1   What negative impact might it have on the organization or the customer? 'Weight' this impact, awarding points out of five where 5 = greatest impact, and 1 = least.

2   How likely is this particular consequence? Award points out of one for probability, where 1 = certain and 0 = impossible.

Identified risk	Impact	Probability	Total

Calculate the total risk by multiplying out.

What action might you take to reduce these risks?

A word of caution: this technique is not objective and absolute; it necessarily involves judgement. So if you want to use it to persuade people of your arguments for or against a particular option, it's important to bring them in on how you arrived at your conclusions. Talk them through the rationale, show them the calculations, and recognize that other people may have different opinions as to the likelihood or otherwise of any consequences.

Costs and benefits

The only reason for undertaking any kind of process improvement or re-design activity is to generate returns for the organization. In order to assess the viability of the improvement, you therefore need to assess what returns it will bring the organization.

Quality is achieved by improvement of the process. Improvement of the process increases uniformity of output of product, reduces rework and mistakes, reduces waste of manpower, machine-time, and materials and thus increases output with less effort. Other benefits ... are lower costs, better competitive position, and happier people on the job, and more jobs, through better competitive position of the company.

(W.E. Deming, 1982)

PRIORITIZATION GRID

A simple technique may help you begin to prioritize your choices. Figure 34 represents the ease (or otherwise) of implementation; and the extent to which the option will deliver benefits.

ACTIVITY 61

Review your options, and plot them all on the grid according to **how much benefit they will bring**, and **how easy they are likely to be to implement**.

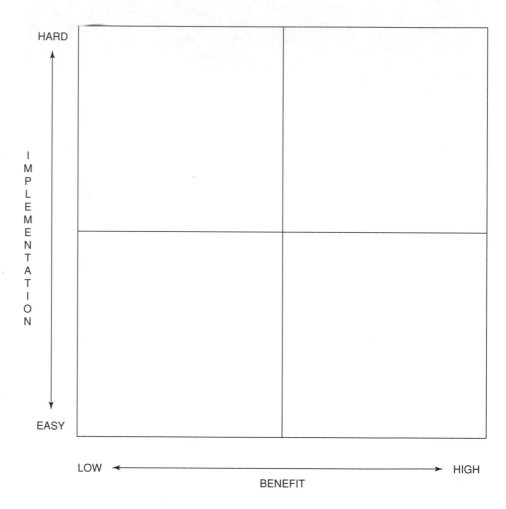

Figure 34   Prioritization grid

Options falling into the 'high benefit' and 'easy to implement' quarter are obvious 'easy wins' for your process. Those falling into the 'high benefit' and 'hard to implement' quarter may still be worth while, but need more careful planning and assessment.

However, before implementing both these types of improvement, do check that each improvement:

- can be implemented independently of other improvements (some may only be possible in conjunction with other steps, which may be harder to implement)
- will not have adverse consequences for other high benefit options, or for other processes in the organization

COST-BENEFIT ANALYSIS

For high benefit options that may be more difficult to implement, you may need to investigate the costs and benefits in greater detail. Cost-benefit analysis is a kind of profit-and-loss account, weighing up those factors that can be quantified in financial terms – the financial benefits (savings or revenue) you anticipate or actually make from the improvement; and the total cost of the improvement. This may be expressed as a total sum:

Financial
benefit from   LESS   Cost of
improvement   improvement   = Gains

or as a ratio:

$$\frac{\text{Financial benefit}}{\text{Cost of improvement}} = \begin{array}{c} \text{Return on each £1} \\ \text{invested (ROI)} \end{array}$$

So all you have to do to calculate the gains or the return on investment is work out total financial benefit, do the same for total costs, and complete the relevant calculation.

Working out these totals, however, may involve some detective work and some informed guesses or assumptions, similar to those an accountant makes when apportioning depreciation. Financial benefits from any improvement may extend over a period of time, so the calculation also needs to make allowances for this.

For example, winning one extra supermarket customer may be worth an average £40 per week. The financial benefit if your improvement gains you this one customer are much more than £40, however. They are multiplied by the number of times the customer is likely to spend that £40 – and how long you keep them. If the average customer shops at the same supermarket fifty weeks a year, and remains loyal for an average of ten years, your figures could look like this:

£40 per week x 50 weeks' shopping = £2000 per year
£2000 x 10 years = £20 000

Winning a single new customer may be worth as much as £20 000 to the supermarket.

Costs should include the costs of researching your improvement option, planning, implementation and new equipment or tools; training or any additional rewards or incentives – as well as the cost of any evaluation efforts. It is also worth remembering that, however beneficial a change may ultimately be, performance immediately afterwards is likely to be worse until people learn how to 'work up' to its potential.

CASE STUDY

To take a very simple example, one team was considering a franking machine to speed up the handling of bulk mailings. They anticipated that the machine would last three years before it needed to be replaced. Their costs looked like this:

BENEFITS	£benefit	£cost
Time saved preparing post: 20 minutes per day x 5 days per week x 52 weeks per year x 3 years at £10 per hour (A)	2600	
COSTS		
Researching options: 16 hours total at £20 per hour		320
Negotiating deal and service contract: 1 hour at £20 per hour		20
Cost of equipment		450
Logo stamp		50
Service agreement (assuming 3 years at £85 per year)		255
Costs total (B)		1095
GAINS therefore over 3 years (A – B)	**£1505**	

ACTIVITY 62

With your team, brainstorm all the possible benefits and costs of one of your improvement options. Write each on a separate Post-it™.

Next, work out the actual values. Start with the benefits. Consider each Post-it™ in order, and calculate what is involved. When you are sure you have considered everything, transfer it to a flip chart page, showing how you arrived at this figure (as in the case study above).

Now do the same for the costs, on a fresh flip chart page.

Calculate the gains.

NON-FINANCIAL COSTS AND BENEFITS

While some costs and benefits may be readily quantifiable, strictly financial measures may be harder to assign for others – improvement to employee morale or reputation when a process hits target, for example, or the loss of employee trust and co-operation that may follow after redundancies. Yet these factors clearly may have a great influence on the way the process delivers its output for the organization and for customers. So they cannot be ignored.

One way of beginning to quantify these involves asking 'so what?' every time a non-financial cost or benefit is identified – and to keep on asking 'so what?' until you arrive at a more quantifiable consequence. For example, one non-financial cost may be the loss of good employee relations. So what? So people are not so co-operative. So what? So they don't do more than they absolutely have to. So what? So they don't stay late to finish jobs. So what? So the job rate per day goes down. You may be able to anticipate the reduction, and you probably already have the average value of a job; calculating the cost of this change is therefore a question of multiplying the reduction by the job value.

Alternatively, you can use a similar technique to the one you used for risk assessment. What area will the costs or benefits affect, and how important is this? Consider in particular what they contribute to your customer output, and the organization's aims, objectives and values. Weight each non-financial cost or benefit as before, awarding 5 for very important, and 1 for not important. Next, rate the impact of the costs or benefits on this area, awarding 5 for very high impact and 1 for little impact. Multiply the two to create a composite score for each non-financial element, then rank costs and benefits separately in order of importance.

Remember, as with the risk assessment, this technique is a question of judgement. The weighting and the ranking may be quite different from different perspectives – your team may assign a different value from you – so again, you will need to show others how you arrived at the comparative scores, and recognize that they may not necessarily agree with you.

Review your non-financial costs and benefits, and try to quantify them using either of the above techniques.

How does this help you to evaluate your options?

If you are able to assign financial values, revise your cost-benefit analysis to take account of these.

Criteria for success

By now, you should be clarifying what is involved in each option, and the likely implications for the organization. You are therefore in a much better position to decide the basis on which you will make your final comparison and selection of the options you want to implement.

WHAT CRITERIA?

To make the choice as objective as possible, the comparison should be based on specific criteria (agreed with the team where appropriate). These criteria should state:

- what you expect any improvement to achieve
- how you will know when any improvement is successful

They may include any of the dimensions your process needs to develop, as identified on the process scorecard. They may also incorporate any constraints (such as utilizing existing equipment); and what the process must deliver for the organization and for the customer.

For example, a successful improvement might need to:

- be acceptable to staff
- optimize existing resources
- deliver greatest estimated benefit
- be easy to implement

Once you have specified the criteria that determine whether an improvement option is successful, you can use them as yardsticks against which to assess your improvement options.

WEIGHTED CRITERIA WORKSHEET

The criteria are the basis of a weighted criteria worksheet, which applies the weighting principle we have already used for risk assessment and non-financial factors. However, in order to compare different options, the chart is set out slightly differently. The criteria are written down the left-hand side of the page. The remainder of the page is divided into columns representing the number of options you are considering PLUS one.

'Weight' the criteria to indicate how important they are to your solution (with 10 = VERY important; and 1 = NOT important). The 'weighting' for each criterion is entered in the appropriate box in the first column (nearest the criteria). The remaining columns are labelled with your options. Draw diagonal lines extending from the bottom-left corner to top-right corner of each box in the options columns. You'll end up with something like Figure 35.

CRITERIA the improvement must:	Weight	Option A	Option B	Option C	Option D
Be acceptable to staff	7				
Optimize existing resources	9				
Deliver greatest financial benefit	10				
Be easy to implement	5				
TOTALS					

Figure 35   Drawing the worksheet and weighting criteria

Next, score each option against each criterion; how far does this option deliver this criterion? Write the score in the top triangle of the box underneath each option. For example (although we have only shown one option completed here, for the sake of simplicity) you might end up with something like Figure 36.

CRITERIA the improvement must:	Weight	Option A	Option B	Option C	Option D
Be acceptable to staff	7	6			
Optimize existing resources	9	8			
Deliver greatest financial benefit	10	6			
Be easy to implement	5	2			
TOTALS					

Figure 36   Scoring each option

Do the same for each option. Next, multiply the score for that criterion by the weight it carries, and write the result in the lower triangle. For example, 'acceptable to staff' was weighted at 7; option A scored 6 on this criterion; so the score entered in the bottom right of the box is 7 x 6 = 42. Again showing just one option for the sake of simplicity, you might end up with something like Figure 37.

Complete the calculations for all options, and add up the scores. The option with the highest total is the one that best meets your criteria. (Of course, the usual cautions apply. Completing the weighted criteria worksheet together with your team may help to broaden the acceptance of your final decision.)

CRITERIA the improvement must:	Weight	Option A	Option B	Option C	Option D
Be acceptable to staff	7	6 42			
Optimize existing resources	9	8 72			
Deliver greatest financial benefit	10	6 60			
Be easy to implement	5	2 10			
TOTALS		184			

Figure 37   Calculating total scores

ACTIVITY 64

Prepare a weighted criteria worksheet assessing your improvement options.

Planning implementation

Once the decision is made about which options you are going to pursue, you may feel as though you are nearly there. But implementation will need careful planning if the improvements are to achieve what you hope. And as you implement your plan, you'll need to keep checking that you're achieving the results you wanted, that you're on target. Process analysis involves a continuous cycle, as we saw in Section 1.

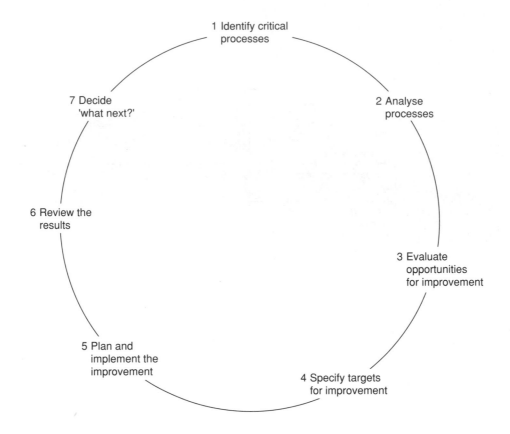

Figure 38   Process management framework

MILESTONES AND REVIEW POINTS

First of all, in order to ensure that your improvement delivers the benefits you want, it's important to state what you want it to achieve. You may already have identified the key **criteria** (from your weighted criteria worksheet); now try to specify these in measurable terms. (For example, in the weighted criteria worksheet above, we listed 'optimize existing resources': you now need to specify which resources and how they will be optimized.) Then you can identify **milestones** or interim targets along the path towards this goal.

Start off by defining the major steps required to implement your process improvement. (A macro process map may help you here.) List these major steps on separate flipchart pages. Next, decide your milestones or interim targets for each major step. How will you know when the step is complete? What do you expect the process to deliver once the step is complete? Use the criteria you identified for the weighted criteria worksheet, and any relevant measures you identified in Section 5, and try to quantify these as far as possible. Write the milestones up underneath the step headings.

ACTION PLAN

Now, list in order, all the activities involved in each step; it may help to write each on a separate Post-it™ at first, so that you can rearrange them and add activities as you think things through. When you think you have identified all the individual activities involved, you can work through the list and assign responsibility, resources and time so that each activity actually happens. Action planning involves deciding:

- **WHAT** to do
- **WHO** will do it
- What **RESOURCES** they need to do it
- **WHEN** it should be done

Reviews

Don't forget to include reviews in your action plan. For each major activity or major step, you will need to compare progress against the milestones you have identified, to check that you are on target. Bear in mind your organization's preferred time horizons; how soon will you be expected to demonstrate results? Experts caution against premature evaluation; it always takes time to 'work up' to any change. Allow for this 'working up' time when planning when and what you will report to senior management (if they are involved). But you will need to keep your finger on the pulse as the improvement project progresses.

Refer back to the work you did in Section 5 on measures and methods of gathering and analysing data, for help in determining what information you will need, how it will be collected, and how it will be presented, to facilitate review and any subsequent adjustment required to your plan or methods.

ACTIVITY 65

Use the action planning form below to plan the major steps and individual activities involved in implementing your improvement – including reviews and the milestones along the way.

MAJOR STEP			
Milestones:			
WHAT must be done?	**WHO** will do it?	**WHAT** **RESOURCES** do they need?	**WHEN** will it be done (and how long will it take

Figure 39   Action planner

GANTT CHARTS

If your schedule is complex, or involves several interdependent activities, you may find a **Gantt chart** useful. This displays the blocks of time for each activity in a visual format, making it easier to spot what happens when, and how the activities flow one from another.

All the activities are listed separately down the left-hand side of the page, and the dates for completion across the top of the page. Then you block in the time allocated for each activity – in sequence – starting with the first activity. The following Gantt chart (Figure 40) shows the activities required to implement the improvement option of one team who had decided to install a franking machine for bulk mailings.

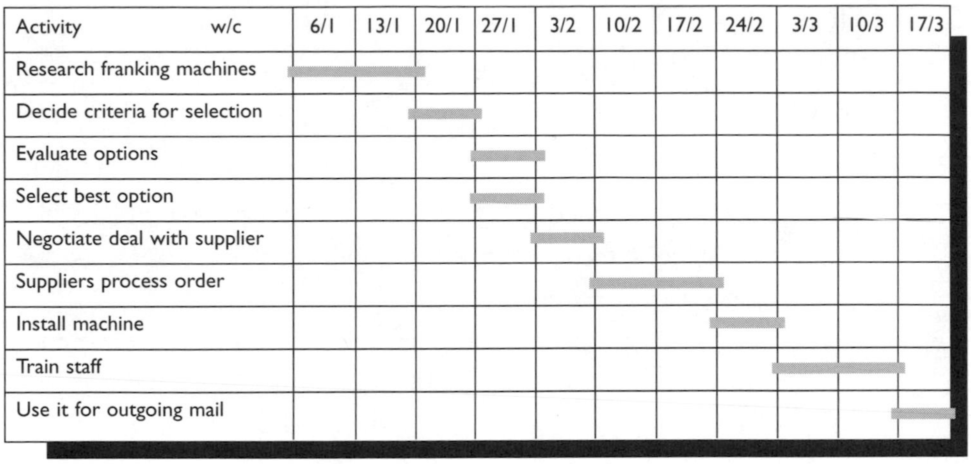

Activity w/c	6/1	13/1	20/1	27/1	3/2	10/2	17/2	24/2	3/3	10/3	17/3
Research franking machines	▨▨	▨									
Decide criteria for selection			▨								
Evaluate options				▨							
Select best option				▨							
Negotiate deal with supplier					▨						
Suppliers process order						▨	▨				
Install machine								▨			
Train staff									▨	▨	
Use it for outgoing mail											▨

Figure 40

You can see that the implementation is planned to start in the week commencing 6 January, and the new machine should be installed, and staff trained to use it by the week commencing 17 March. (The timings on this example are very generous, and no activities are concurrent, in order to illustrate the principle more clearly. Your own examples are likely to include overlapping activities and tighter scheduling.)

ACTIVITY 66

Draw up a Gantt chart to co-ordinate the timings of activities in your action plan.

CONTINGENCIES

Projects rarely go entirely to plan; there's always some unexpected occurrence that may throw your plan out. However, some difficulties can be anticipated – for example, where deadlines are tight, you might anticipate failing to keep to schedule; or where activities are sequential, delays in one will obviously lead to delays in subsequent activities. So it makes sense to anticipate and plan for contingencies.

Take another look through your list of activities in Activity 65 and identify where potential problems are likely to have greatest effect on the improvement effort. What kinds of things may go wrong? How could you deal with this? Anticipate 'best case' and 'worst case' scenarios, and schedule and plan for both. And don't forget to amend your action plan, and your cost-benefit analysis accordingly.

ACTIVITY 67

Summarize the above section by listing the key elements that a good contingency plan should cover.

DON'T JUST PLAN – DO IT!

Planning and preparation can only get you so far. Unless you implement the improvement, you will not gain the benefits. So don't just plan what you're going to do – do it. (And then review to analyse how it went, and loop back to identify further opportunities for improvement, and start the cycle again.)

Summary

The existing **organizational context** – its culture and values, its structure and technology, its resources and time horizons – will determine the feasibility of any improvement. It is therefore essential to consider what factors may support or hinder the improvements you propose, to establish their feasibility, and what additional action may be required to support them.

Any change is likely to have some **risk** attached – experts suggest that the degree of risk is directly related to the degree of change. So it makes sense to anticipate the likelihood of any negative consequences, and plan to overcome these.

Having clarified what may be involved in each option, the next step is to estimate the likely **costs and benefits**. A formal cost-benefit analysis may be required for some improvement projects to secure approval; although not all benefits can be quantified in strictly financial terms, and it is equally important to consider non-financial costs and benefits, which may be fundamental to the success or otherwise of the process.

The next step is to specify the **criteria for success**, and to evaluate each option against these criteria. What must the improvement deliver for the process? How will you know it has been successful? The weighted criteria worksheet may help to clarify the comparisons between options where there is no obvious choice.

The final stage before implementation is to **plan** every detail of implementation – WHAT you will do (including reviews), WHO will do it, what RESOURCES they need, and WHEN they will do it. A **Gantt chart** may help to keep track of schedules, especially where timings are concurrent or interdependent. Then it is simply a question of DOING it – and cycling back to the beginning of the process evaluation loop once more.

Summary

This workbook has now taken you through the basic ideas and techniques involved with managing processes in organizations. Together with Workbook 4, *Customer Focus* it sets out the key ideas, models and tools that make up the key role 'Manage Activities' at Level 4.

You should now be able to:

■ understand what business process management relates to and impacts on other management ideas such as TQM, and continuous improvement

■ understand the relationship between business processes and other functions such as organizational systems and human resource management

■ use the tools and techniques to improve processes in your organization

As a practical guide its purpose is not just to inform you, and help you to acquire the appropriate knowledge, but to help you to develop understanding of the issues involved in the implementation of ideas and tools in a real working environment.

Recommended reading

Bell, D., McBride, P. and Wilson, G., (1994) *Managing Quality*, Institute of Management, Butterworth-Heinemann

British Standards Institute (1994) BS EN ISO9000, BSI

Carr, D.K. and Johansson, H.J., (1995) *Best Practices in Re-engineering: what works and what doesn't in the re-engineering process*, McGraw-Hill

Champy, J., (1995) *Re-engineering Management*, Harper Collins

Covey, S.R., (1992) *The Seven Habits of Highly Effective People*, Simon & Shuster

Davenport, T.H., (1993) *Process Innovation: re-engineering work through information technology*, Harvard Business School Press

Davenport, T.H. and Short, J.E., (1990) 'The new industrial engineering: information technology and business process redesign', *Sloan Management Review*, Summer, pp.11–27

Deming, W.E., (1982) *Quality, Productivity and Competitive Position, MIT*

Edwards, C.C., (1995) 'Re-engineering: the critical success factors', *Management Services*, December, pp.26–27

Fowler, E. and Graves, P., (1995) M*anaging an Effective Operation,* Institute of Management, Butterworth-Heinemann

Gilbert, T.F., (1978) *Human Competence*, McGraw-Hill

Glassop, L., (1995) *The Road to Quality*, Australian Institute of Management NSW Training Centre, Prentice Hall Australia Pty

Hammer (1990) 'Re-engineering work: don't automate, obliterate', *Harvard Business Review*, July–August, pp.104–112

Hammer and Champy, J. (1993) *Engineering the Corporation: A manifesto for business revolution*, Nicolas Brearley

Hannagan, T., (1995) *Management Concepts and Practices*, Pitman Publishing

Harrington, H.J., (1991) *Business Process Improvement: the breakthrough strategy for total quality*, productivity and competitiveness, McGraw-Hill

Harrison, P. amd D'Vaz, G., (1995) *Business Process Re-engineering*, Management Direction series, Institute of Management

Institute of Management, (1995) *Managing Operations*, Competent Manager series

Johansen, R. and Swigart, R., (1994) *Upsizing the Individual in the Downsized Organization*, Century

Kanji, G.K. and Asher, M., (1996) *100 methods for Total Quality Management*, Sage Publications

Kubler-Ross, E., (1989) *On Death and Dying*, Routledge

Macdonald, J., (1995) *Understanding Total Quality Management in a Week*, Institute of Management, Hodder & Stoughton

Macdonald, J., (1995) *Understanding Business Process Re-engineering in a Week*, Institute of Management, Hodder & Stoughton

McGregor, D., (1960) *The Human Side of Enterprise*, McGraw-Hill

Maull, R.S., Weaver, A.M., Childe, S.J., Smart, P.A. and Bennett, J., (1995) 'Current issues in business process re-engineering', *International Journal of Operations and Production Management*, **15** (11), pp.37–52

O'Neill, B. and Moult, G., (1994) *Managing in Context*, Competent Manager series, Institute of Management, May

Parker, N. and Harrison, P., (1995) *Benchmarking*, Management Directions series, Institute of Management

Smith, I., (1994) *Meeting Customer Needs*, Institute of Management, Butterworth-Heinemann

Stamps, D., (1996) 'Corporate anorexia', *Training*, February, pp.24–30

Thomas, M., (1994) 'What you need to know about: business process re-engineering', *Personnel Management*, January, pp.28–31

Towers, S., (1993) 'Business process re-engineering – lessons for success', *Management Services*, August, pp.10–12

Tucker, M., (1996) *Successful Process Management in a Week*, Institute of Management, Hodder & Stoughton

Wellins and Rick, (1995) 'Taking account of the human factor', *People Management*, **21**, 19 October

Wilkinson, A., Redman, T. and Snape, E., (1993) *Quality and the Manager*, Institute of Management research report

About the Institute of Management

The mission of the Institute of Management (IM) is to promote the development, exercise and recognition of professional management.

The IM is the leading professional organization for managers. Its efforts and resources are devoted to ensuring the continuing development and success of its members.

At the forefront of management standards, the IM provides a range of services for its members. These include flexible training programmes and a unique range of support services such as career counselling, enquiry and research facilities and preferential prices on IM publications and other IM products.

Further details about the Institute of Management may be obtained from:

Institute of Management
Management House
Cottingham Road
Corby
Northants
NN17 1TT

Telephone 01536 204222

We need your views

We really need your views in order to make the Institue of Management Open Learning Programme an even better learning tool for you. Please take time out to complete and return this questionnaire to Tessa Gingell, Pergamon Open Learning, Linacre House, Jordan Hill, Oxford OX2 8DP.

Name:...

Address:...

....

Title of workbook:..

If applicable, please state which qualification you are studying for. If not, please describe what study you are undertaking, and with which organization or college:

....

Please grade the following out of 10 (10 being extremely good, 0 being extremely poor):

Content: ....   Suitability for ability level: ....

Readability: ....   Qualification coverage: ....

What did you particularly like about this workbook?

....

Are there any features you disliked about this workbook? Please identify them.

....

Are there any errors we have missed?
If so, please state page number: ....

How are you using the material? For example, as an open learning course, as a reference resource, as a training resource, etc.

....

How did you hear about the Institue of Management Open Learning Programme?:

Word of mouth: Through my tutor/trainer: Mailshot:

Other (please give details):..

Many thanks for your help in returning this form.

Institute of Management Open Learning Programme

This programme comprises seventeen workbooks, each on a core management topic with the latest management thinking, as well as a *User Guide* and a *Mentor Guide*.

Designed for self study through open learning, the workbooks cover all management experience from team building to budgeting, from the skills of self management to manage strategically for organizational success.

TITLE	ISBN	Price
The Influential Manager	0 7506 3662 9	£22.50
Managing Yourself	0 7506 3661 0	£22.50
Getting the Right People to Do the Right Job	0 7506 3660 2	£22.50
Understanding Business Process Management	0 7506 3659 9	£22.50
Customer Focus	0 7506 3663 7	£22.50
Getting TQM to Work	0 7506 3664 5	£22.50
Leading from the Front	0 7506 3665 3	£22.50
Improving Your Organization's Success	0 7506 3666 1	£22.50
Project Management	0 7506 3667 X	£22.50
Budgeting and Financial Control	0 7506 3668 8	£22.50
Effective Financial and Resource Management	0 7506 3669 6	£22.50
Developing Yourself and Your Staff	0 7506 3670 X	£22.50
Building a High Performance Team	0 7506 3671 8	£22.50
The New Model Leader	0 7506 3672 6	£22.50
Making Rational Decisions	0 7506 3673 4	£22.50
Communication	0 7506 3674 2	£22.50
Successful Information Management	0 7506 3675 0	£22.50
User Guide	0 7506 3676 9	£22.50
Mentor Guide	0 7506 3677 7	£22.50
Full set of workbooks plus *Mentor Guide* and *User Guide*	0 7506 3359 X	£370.00

To order: *(Please quote ISBNs when ordering)*

- College Orders: 01865 314333
- Account holders: 01865 314301
- Individual Purchases: 01865 314627

(Please have credit card details ready)

For further information or to request a full series brochure, please contact:

Tessa Gingell on 01865 314477